# GOOD LESSONS from BAD EXAMPLES

DEAN H. GARRISON

# GOOD LESSONS
## from
# BAD EXAMPLES

DEAN H. GARRISON

**BROADMAN PRESS**
Nashville, Tennessee

4251-86
ISBN: 0-8054-5186-2

Unless otherwise noted, Scripture quotations are from the King
James Version of the Bible.

Quotations marked NEB are from *The New English Bible*.
Copyright © The Delegates of the Oxford University Press and the
Syndics of the Cambridge University Press, 1961, 1970. Reprinted
by permission.

Dewey Decimal Classification: 220.92
Subject heading: BIBLE—BIOGRAPHY

Library of Congress Catalog Card Number: 81-68363
Printed in the United States of America

# Contents

# Preface

There is a tendency for most of us to become interested in stories of people and events which describe noble acts and their usual happy endings. "And they lived happily everafter."

This tendency exists because, in our own striving for good, we are encouraged by those who have achieved right ends for their lives, having faced and conquered problems with which we can identify. This is especially important for those of us who have endeavored to pattern our lives after the Holy Bible. We live and breathe with the heroes of the faith.

The widespread knowledge of these inspired stories has given rise to common expressions which are linked with the specific characteristics of a person. These sayings have become a form of "shorthand" which reminds us of an attractive trait or virtue. For instance, we think of "the wisdom of Solomon" or "the patience of Job." Thus, it is possible that our knowledge of another's success in coping with problems and tragedies can give us a degree of encouragement.

Because the Bible record is not contrived, the study of its heroes or villains is not clouded by any prejudice to make them look good or bad. This statement is supported by the fact that the foibles and sins of the "righteous" are vividly recorded in the Word of God—Noah drunk in his tent, Abraham caught in lies, Rebecca and Jacob conniving to steal a birthright, David committing adultery and indirect murder, James and John jealously and politically vying for first and second places in Jesus' kingdom, Peter's cursing and denial of his Lord, Paul and Barnabas's heated disagreement over John Mark, and many more.

So, the biblical narrative was written with the express purpose of presenting correct information about historical events and spiritual phenomena associated with those events.

Since there is informative and inspirational truth to be gleaned from stories of the "good" people in the Bible, it is likewise true that the accounts of misdeeds and even crimes of "bad" people could also serve for our instruction—and also teach us to "go thóu and do" exactly the opposite!

As we study a few of these unrighteous characters, let's notice the wrong deeds perpetrated and some of the predisposing conditions which may have prompted such sin and malice. Second, let's view the manner in which others responded to these villains. It is difficult, for instance, to explore the lives of Saul and Absalom and not be impressed with David's responses to the severe problems he encountered with those enemies.

Third, insight can come from the subsequent action which characterized God's position in the matter. Of course, our perspective on right and wrong is only partial and at best a distortion of God's view. His judgment, of course, stems from an absolute point of view. However, in many instances there is certain fundamental agreement between God's conception and "righteous" persons' opinions of what constitutes evil conduct.

The Bible is laden with many examples of wrongdoing both against God and man. The bad examples described in these pages give us a variety of personality types drawn from a period of time spanning almost two thousand years, from the beginning of the Hebrew nation to the Apostolic Era of the early church in the Book of Acts.

The beginning of each chapter will develop the historical setting and provide a smooth transition from one character to the next. The remainder of each chapter will set forth the person's biography accurately abstracted from the biblical account. I will analyze as much as possible the true character of the individual and sift the internal and external forces which gave rise to his bad behavior. In addition to the Bible, I made extensive use of secular history in order to complement the narrative. The purpose of this work is to study the darker side of biblical personages and the effect their conduct had on their contemporaries—and ultimately on many of us.

I have chosen to write about the bad people of the Scriptures for three reasons: (1) Their stories reveal many evil deeds which appear surprisingly necessary to the unfolding of God's plan, (2) Their lives provide many object lessons, especially in cases where the main character is in a position of leadership, and (3) It is instructive for us to observe how others apparently missed God's eternal remedy—so we won't.

I trust that we will learn good lessons from bad examples.

DEAN H. GARRISON

# 1
# Esau

## The Sale of a Soul

The first book in the Bible is the record of numerous beginnings. Genesis contains the story of creation from the organization of the physical universe to the forming of the first human, Adam. Adam and his mate Eve were presented with some choices, and upon making the wrong ones introduced sin into the experience of mankind. The first quarter of Genesis covers a period of about two thousand years. In addition to creation, it tells the epic story of the Flood, which only Noah and seven members of his family survived, and the subsequent growth, diversity, and extensive distribution of the race.

During this time, God interacted with his creation, but it was not until the appearance of the man Abraham that he seems to focus attention upon one individual with the purpose of carrying out a specific long-range plan for the destiny of millions of people.

God promised Abraham that his descendants would become a large nation and that the ancient land of Canaan would be the territory where this nation would settle. God chose him because he was a righteous man and because he believed wholeheartedly in what God had promised. Fulfillment of the promise of the land in Canaan as a homeland began when God spoke to Abraham and directed him to move from his family home at Ur in southeast Mesopotamia to Haran, six hundred miles to the northwest. Among the family members who made this trip were his father Terah, his nephew Lot, and his wife Sarah, who was also his half-sister. After a short stay in Haran, where his father died, Abraham moved southwest to the city of Shechem about forty-five miles north of Hebron. After residing in various places in and out of Canaan, this nomadic family finally settled near Hebron.

By this time, Abraham had acquired enough material wealth and servants that he became a major force in the area, not only in the defense of his own property but also as a defender of others. On one of these occasions he rescued his nephew Lot who was living in Sodom. Lot was carried off, along with his possessions, when that city was captured by a confederacy of marauding kings.

The other part of God's promise that Abraham would father a great nation seemed remote to Abraham and Sarah, because they were both getting older and up to now had had no children. In their impatience, they decided that Abraham should take Sarah's Egyptian slave girl Hagar as his wife, believing that this would help God with his plan. Just as was hoped, Hagar had a child, but, as might be expected, neither Sarah nor God were satisfied with the results. Subsequently, Hagar and her son Ishmael were ejected from the family, and God proceeded with his original plan that Sarah should be the mother in the next step of the great-nation promise. It is more than interesting that in a shadowy way God fulfilled through Ishmael, the rejected son, his promise about Abraham's descendants in that we now have that large mass of persons who are identified as Arabs, and that the fierce contention over the area of Canaan between the two branches of Abraham's family continues to this day.

A dozen or more years went by, and Abraham and Sarah, both old and past the time when couples normally have children, were informed by God through three visiting messengers that within a year they would have a son. True to the prediction, a son was born to them the following year and they named him Isaac. Isaac, which means "one who laughs," alludes to Abraham's and Sarah's amusement at the announcement that they, in their old age, would possibly become parents. Upon the birth of the infant, it became clear to Abraham that Isaac was God's chosen one through whom he would carry out the promises. Thirty-seven years after Isaac's birth, Sarah died. Although Abraham had more children, Isaac was the only offspring born to the two of them.

Years passed and it became Abraham's concern that his son Isaac should marry and thus continue the family line. Because of the seriousness of the decision, and because all of the local Canaanite women were pagan, Abraham instructed a trusted servant to retrace his own journey back to his home at Haran to seek a wife for Isaac. Abraham assured his servant that God would reward their faith and provide a suitable bride from among his own relatives. Abraham's action may well have been prompted by the seemingly hapless results of his relationship with the outsider Hagar. The servant was successful and returned with the beautiful Rebecca. The marriage appears to have been satisfactory to all concerned. The acceptable close kinship was that of a first cousin once removed (i.e., Isaac's uncle was Rebecca's grandfather).

The account of our first villain began with the marriage and family life of Isaac and Rebecca. This couple was childless for nearly twenty years. Finally, as a result of Isaac's sincere prayer, God allowed Rebecca to conceive. Even before the twins Esau and Jacob were born, the overactivity of the babies in her womb caused Rebecca to seek an explanation from God. God's words to her indicated that her womb contained two nations, that the two would go separate ways, that one would be the stronger and the older of the two would be servant to the younger.

During delivery of the twins, the first to emerge was Esau. This name, which means "hairy," was chosen because of the extraordinary amount of hair which covered most of his body. Immediately following the boy Jacob was born; in fact, his hand had a grasp upon his brother's foot as the births progressed. When the two grew up, Esau became proficient in hunting and was very much of an outdoorsman, while Jacob chose to stay close to home and appears to have been a more gentle and settled person. Isaac was very fond of his son Esau because he was a hunter and on occasion would provide his father with a favorite meat dish. Rebecca seemed to favor Jacob, possibly because he remained near the family tent and was available to be of help to his mother.

One day, perhaps while Jacob was assisting with the cooking in the absence of their parents, Esau came in tired and hungry, insisting that Jacob feed him. His hunger was so intense that, upon Jacob's suggestion, he agreed to exchange his rights as the firstborn for some of the red soup Jacob was preparing. Believing that if he did not eat at once he would certainly die and then the birthright would be of no value, he took an oath and relinquished those rights and privileges which normally fell to the oldest son.

Ancient custom determined that the family name

and any significant titles be carried and transferred through the son born first. Also, a double portion of property would be inherited and, in a religious family, the oldest son would act as priest for the household. Esau's father Isaac was wealthy by local standards because, although Abraham was still alive, he had probably turned most of his property over to Isaac. It is difficult to understand why at the time Esau thought so little of at least the material advantages of these rights, that he traded them away for such a small thing as a meal.

A few years later, while residing at Beersheba, God spoke to Isaac in the same manner in which he had spoken to his father Abraham. God reiterated that he would be blessed with many descendants. Isaac was well aware of the great pains his father had taken to assure that he was provided a wife from among his own people and probably was beginning to think about plans for a suitable partner for his son Esau. But this was not to be, because at the age of forty Esau married not one, but two women from among their pagan neighbors. This was most upsetting to Isaac and Rebecca because Esau had bypassed their role in the decision and had deliberately disobeyed them by marrying into a heathen nation.

Now Isaac was old, his eyesight was failing, and he knew it was time to bestow his patriarchal blessing upon his son Esau. He planned to do this with the hope that the promises might yet be fulfilled through Esau in spite of his poor choice of wives. This was similar to Abraham's wish earlier that Ishmael might have been in that position. Isaac seems to have had no knowledge of the bad bargain that Esau had made with Jacob many years before. It also appears that this event had been long-forgotten by Esau.

To set the mood, Isaac instructed Esau to go out into the wild and kill a deer, prepare his father's favorite venison dish, and bring the meal to him. This then would be the occasion when the eldest son would receive the blessing. Obediently, Esau got his hunting equipment and went to the fields. It seems that Rebecca overheard her husband's instructions to Esau and immediately set about a cruel plan which, when carried out, would hurt both of them very deeply.

Unlike Isaac, Rebecca probably knew about the earlier sale of the birthright and, since she favored Jacob, was now presented with a golden opportunity to complete the transaction of getting the right blessing to go to the wrong son. Because there was no time to hunt deer, and besides Jacob was no hunter, Rebecca and Jacob slaughtered a tame animal from their own flock and hurriedly prepared the meal which Jacob would present to his father while passing himself off as Esau. In order to assure success concerning the identity of the one serving the meal, Jacob wore some animal skins on his hands and arms and on the back of his neck. This was essential since Esau was a hairy man, for without it Isaac's probable identification attempt by touch would expose the entire hoax.

Jacob then presented himself to his father, claiming to be Esau and taking credit for hunting and cooking the meal. Jacob and his mother were a little too efficient, and this caused Isaac to question the speed with which the animal was located and downed. Jacob displayed the height of effrontery by crediting God with "putting it in his way." Even though Isaac also questioned the voice discrepancy, he finally seemed satisfied after feeling Jacob's hands which had been disguised with the animal skins.

After the meal, Isaac proceeded to bless the son whom he believed to be the rightful heir. The blessing included the prospect of material benefit as well as the prophecy that people would serve him, including his own brother, and finally, "a curse upon those who curse you; a blessing upon those who bless you!" (Gen. 27:29, NEB). Pronouncements of this kind in Scripture were general well-wishes to the recipient but also had, at times, specific prophetic implications. Although Jacob did turn out ultimately to be the one for whom this blessing was meant, he and his scheming mother could take no credit, since their part in the process had executed a cruel trick upon both Isaac and Esau.

About the time Jacob made his exit, unsuspecting Esau came in to serve his prepared meal to the

similarly unsuspecting Isaac. It did not take very long
for them to discover that they both had been duped.
Esau now recalled having been tricked out of his
birthright earlier, and in anger lamented that this
follow-up move was in character for a man whose name
meant "supplanter." There followed a great deal of
crying and begging on Esau's part, but to no avail—the
blessing would stand. However, after much pleading,
Isaac did pronounce a blessing of sorts upon Esau
which contained mostly negative opposites to what had
been given on Jacob's behalf. Only the last part was
encouraging because it spoke of a time in the future
when Esau would break the yoke of his brother's
domination.

The insult and humiliation caused Esau to hate his
brother and to begin planning his murder. He decided
to wait until his father died so that he would have a free
hand to get his revenge. When Rebecca discovered this
plan, she persuaded Jacob to flee to her relatives at
Haran and promised that she would send for him when
Esau's anger had cooled. Her approach to Isaac was
quite different; to him she made the point by saying
that she would "just die" if their other son were to
marry a pagan woman as Esau had done. This argu-
ment was so convincing that Isaac called Jacob, blessed
him, and instructed him to travel to the home of
Rebecca's brother Laban and seek a wife from among
his daughters.

Instead of realizing that his brother's departure from Canaan would probably save both their lives, Esau was again angered because of the renewed blessing and because Jacob was being sent away to find himself a wife. When he understood that his parent's dislike for the local women was part of the motive behind Jacob's trip, he promptly went out and married one of Ishmael's daughters. It is in this union that another people, the Edomites, have their origin.

We encounter Esau in this first book of the Bible many years later when he and Jacob met briefly upon the latter's return to Canaan. It now seemed as if Rebecca's prediction—that the passage of time would moderate Esau's anger—was correct, for although Jacob was terrified to face his brother, the meeting was reasonably amicable and they parted without any trouble.

In analyzing Esau's conduct and character, one does not find an out-and-out wicked person. His life seems to be a pathetic picture of a man who, for some reason, lacked the understanding of the worth of a thing. Often, as in the case of Esau, when confronted with a choice between two alternatives, an individual with this weakness allows his physical needs to momentarily overshadow some obvious greater good outside of himself. It was unfortunate for Esau that such a profound outcome resulted from what appeared to him to be a seemingly unimportant choice.

Another act which revealed his lack of appreciation for significant matters was his disregard of the specific wish of his parents that he not select a wife from among a pagan nation. Again, he placed his desire for gratification above a number of more important considerations. Esau was what we might call a profane man because he just did not care about the deeper things of life. The writer of the Book of Hebrews in the New Testament, while expressing encouragement toward holy and noble living, cites Esau as an example of one who was worldly-minded and therefore bargained away much and got in exchange something of little value.

This sad story of Esau depicting poor choices, destructive responses, and disappointing outcomes is a clear instruction of the care with which God expects his human creation to note what is truly important. Esau found it easier to be driven by his shallow wants and feelings than to listen to God, and that was his undoing.

We do not know what finally happened to Esau. We do know that he settled in the region near Mount Seir south and east of the Dead Sea. His descendants survived in this place until AD 70 when the area was conquered by the Romans under Titus. After this event, the Edomites disappeared from history. Their major doom was predicted by at least five of the Old Testament prophets. The Book of Obadiah, written about thirteen hundred years after the time of Esau, is devoted entirely to the all-but-complete destruction of the Edomites for cruel acts committed against Israel. Phrases like "cut off for ever" (v. 10) and "shall be as though they had never been" (v. 17) tell in harsh terms God's judgment on the descendants of Esau, the man who sold his birthright for a mess of pottage.

# 2
# Saul

## The Counsel of a Witch

When Jacob hastily departed his home because of his brother Esau's plan to murder him, he traveled from Beersheba toward Haran. Haran was the city to which Abraham and his father's family had migrated many years earlier and it was the birthplace of Rebecca. Early in the four hundred mile trip he stopped for the night near the city of Luz and, while sleeping out in the open field, dreamed he saw a ladder reaching to heaven. Angels were going up and down the ladder, and the Lord spoke to Jacob reaffirming the promises that had been made to his grandfather Abraham and his father Isaac. Again these referred to a large nation living in Canaan, with such special attention from God that other nations would desire similar blessings. God also assured Jacob that he would return safely to the land he was about to leave. Upon waking, Jacob constructed a stone monument and renamed the place Bethel, which means "house of God."

Jacob continued his journey to Haran. Upon arriving, he located his Uncle Laban and for the next twenty years lived in his home working as a hired man. During this time, Jacob acquired both of Laban's daughters and two servant girls as wives, and to these four women were born eleven sons and one daughter. In addition to his large family, he had gained much wealth in flocks of animals. He and his household departed Haran and headed back toward the Land of Promise. At a place along the way, which Jacob called Peniel because of another encounter there with God, his name was changed to Israel. It was on this return trip that Jacob and Esau met for the last time.

In Canaan, Jacob settled near Shechem, which was the same place where Abraham had stopped when he first entered the land many years earlier. His sons' massacre of the men of Shechem because one of them had violated their sister Dinah caused Jacob to move on to Bethel and finally establish his home near Hebron. It was during this trip that Jacob's favorite wife, Rachel, died while giving birth to Benjamin. Her death occurred near Bethlehem and she was buried there.

In the way that his parents had showed favoritism within the family, Jacob made the same mistake with his son Joseph, Rachel's only other son. This fostered great jealousy among his brothers and resulted in Joseph being sold by them as a slave to Ishmaelites who carried him off to Egypt. While in Egypt, Joseph, having good character and being guided by God, rose to a position of leadership. It was his skillful administration which saved Egypt during a famine and placed him in the peculiar circumstance which resulted in his family being reunited. The famine forced Jacob and the rest of his family to move to Egypt and it was here that this tribe of over seventy persons grew to a large nation over the next four hundred years. (See Ex. 46:26.)

Because of the severe persecution of the children of Israel, they left Egypt under the leadership of Moses, determined to return to the land that had been promised to their forefathers. The census of the time recorded about six hundred thousand men, besides women and children. (See Ex. 12:37.) The group was organized into twelve separate tribes identified according to the names of ten of Israel's twelve sons and two of Joseph's sons born in Egypt. The events of their escape and subsequent wanderings in the wilderness are recorded in the Book of Exodus. In order to avoid hostile peoples, and because this was a prolonged preparation for a difficult future, they followed a very indirect route across the Sinai Desert. The last half of the book details the events surrounding a year's encampment at Mount Sinai. Through Moses, God gave the Ten Commandments, the civil law, and instituted the priesthood which was to be made up of the descendants of Levi, Israel's third son.

Although Moses was a successful leader in bringing the Israelites to the very brink of entry into the land which God had designated as their perpetual homeland, it was Joshua, Moses' military commander, who was chosen to go in to conquer Canaan. Only a few persons had survived the forty years of travel; therefore, the people about to claim the land were mostly those who were born during the wilderness journey.

Joshua's task was to provide military and spiritual leadership, and this he did admirably. Once the land was conquered, it was divided into regions, each belonging to one of the tribes. The Hebrew nation was now a confederacy of twelve fairly independent states held together loosely by their monotheistic beliefs.

For the next three hundred years, a series of local leaders called judges appeared from time to time, filling the role of military deliverers. The hardy generation of those who crossed Sinai had died off and their successors had great difficulty protecting themselves from invading enemies. Many persons had rejected the worship of God and were flirting with idolatry. During this time there were in all thirteen judges who showed themselves effective for God in the protection of his people. A typical cycle would start with a crisis situation occurring during a low point in the spiritual life of the people. In desperate straits, they would call upon God who would then raise up a deliverer. With God's help the revived people were victorious. In the final phase the people forgot God and reverted back to pagan ways.

The Book of Judges closes with a disastrous civil war between the tribe of Benjamin and the rest of the nation. So extensive was the killing of the Benjaminites that only six hundred men survived; all the women and children perished. When the fighting ceased, the Israelites felt great remorse that they had essentially eliminated one of the twelve tribes. Even though six hundred men remained, there were no women left of their own tribe. Also, no Hebrew women of any other tribe were available because of a prohibiting pledge made during the height of the hostilities. On the basis of the technicality that a particular family group from Jabesh-Gilead was not present during the pledging ceremony, women were found who could marry the remaining men of Benjamin and the tribe was saved from extinction. The last sentence of the record of the judges of Israel is an apt closure to this era, expressing the fact that they were leaderless and that "every man did what was right according to his own judgment" (Judg. 21:25, author's translation). During this time, the tribes were involved in civil strife within and confronted by a number of hostile neighbors who seldom missed an opportunity to attack such a weak and vulnerable people.

It was in this state that the people, seeing

surrounding nations led by kings, made the request
that God allow them to have a king who would unify and
lead their nation. Samuel, the last of the judges, was
the spiritual leader, and it was to him that the request
was made. Although he was not in favor of the plan, he
presented it to God. In God's answer, he assured
Samuel that the people's desire for a king was a
rejection not of Samuel's leadership but of the the-
ocracy. God also warned about kings in general and
their first one in particular, explaining that kings tend
to exploit their subjects by requiring service in their
armies and their households and by taking much of the
people's lands and possessions for royal usage. Samuel
went back to the people and presented God's position;
but the people were determined to have a king, so God
gave Samuel permission to appoint one.

Samuel's first meeting with Saul occurred when
some animals had strayed from Saul's father's flock, and
Saul and a servant were sent to find them. After two
days of searching, it was suggested that a man of God
who lived in the region might assist them in locating
their property. Prior to their encounter, God told
Samuel that the man he was about to meet should be
anointed and that as king he would deliver the nation
from the Philistines. Finally they met, and Samuel
explained that the animals had been found, but more
important that Saul had been chosen by God to be king

and deliverer. Saul protested that he was a Benjaminite
of the smallest tribe and that his family was least
among that tribe. The following day, Samuel privately
anointed Saul and sent him home. At the moment of
their parting, Saul received from God "a new heart"
(1 Sam. 10:9, NEB) in order to equip him for the awe-
some task of being Israel's first king.

A short time later Samuel called a meeting at
Mizpah of all the tribes with the purpose of making a
public choice of Saul. A series of lots were cast. The
selection fell to tribe, family, and finally to Saul. Saul
was hiding when the announcement came but when
presented to the people he was accepted and hailed as
king by the majority. He was a head taller than any
other man and appeared to get immediate approval
because it was said that "there was none like Saul in all
Israel" (1 Sam. 10:24, author's translation).

The first military test of the new king's leadership
came as a result of the imminent invasion of Jabesh-
Gilead by the Ammonites. When told of these circumstances, Saul was working out in the fields; he cut up
the oxen he had been plowing with, and sent the pieces
throughout the country with the message that this
would befall the oxen of any man who would not join
Saul and Samuel in the war against the Ammonites.
The response resulted in a readied army of a third of a
million fighting men. An early morning surprise inva-

sion of the enemy camp almost annihilated the Am-
monite forces. So complete was the victory and so
convincing was Saul's leadership that his followers
wanted to kill those few who had not been supportive of
Saul earlier at Mizpah, but Saul prevented this. The
victory celebration was climaxed by the completion of
Saul's investiture as king "in the Lord's presence"
(1 Sam. 10:15, NEB) at Gilgal.

The next military encounter was provoked when
Saul's son Jonathan killed the garrison of a Philistine
outpost at Geba. In retaliation the Philistines prepared
a large force and waited in encampment. The Israelites
were in a difficult position, with some even retreating
east to the other side of the Jordan River. Before Saul
and his army could go into battle, there had to be a
sacrifice of a whole-offering to God, and this could only
be done by Samuel the priest. Because Samuel was
delayed in coming and the people were drifting away,
Saul took it upon himself and performed the rite. Just
as the ceremony was completed Samuel arrived and,
upon discovering what had been done, dismissed all of
Saul's excuses and proceeded to recite God's punishment for his foolish act. He told Saul that his dynasty
would be cut off and that God would select "a man after
his own heart" (1 Sam. 13:14) to be the next king. After
this pronouncement, Samuel departed, leaving Saul to
fight the Philistines. As the stalemate between the two
armies continued, Jonathan and his armor bearer

secretly left Saul and his forces and overran a Philistine post, killing twenty men. This event triggered panic and confusion among the Philistine army and the Israelites were able to soundly defeat them.

It was during the "mopping-up" phase of the fighting that Saul commanded that no soldier should take any food until their vengeance upon the enemy was complete. The punishment for disobeying the order was death. Jonathan, the hero of the day, did not hear his father's foolish prohibition and, being hungry late in the day, ate some honey which he discovered in the woods. As the day ended Saul inquired of God whether or not to pursue the enemy through the night. This time God was silent, and Saul interpreted this as an indication that someone had disobeyed his order about eating. Even after the revelation that it was his own son who had taken food, Saul insisted that the guilty one must die. Finally it was the people who, in spite of obvious insubordination, declared that Saul's order would be annulled. They would not allow Jonathan's heroism to be lost by a monstrous punishment for disobeying a silly order. The ensuing battle brought victory over the Philistines, and the war ended.

True to the people's expectations, Saul was victorious over all his enemies. One day Samuel told Saul that God wanted to punish the Amalekites for their attack on Israel during their Exodus from Egypt. The Amalekites were a fierce marauding band of people descended from the union of Esau and one of his pagan wives. During the wilderness journey, this wandering tribe attacked the rear guard of the children of Israel, mercilessly picking off any stragglers who could not keep up with the main troop. It was now time for God to avenge the deeds of the Amalekites. His instructions were explicit in that Saul was to destroy everyone and everything. This was not to be the usual case of the conqueror taking prisoners and spoils. Saul's fulfillment of God's directive was incomplete. He did kill all the people but he took King Agag alive. When it came to the disposition of the flocks of animals, he saved the best, destroying only that which was useless. Later, Samuel confronted Saul concerning his sparing of the animals. Saul's reply was a list of lame excuses, the most creative of which was that the choice sheep were being kept for sacrifice to the Lord. Once more Samuel pointed out Saul's refusal to obey God's commandments and consequences were to be that the kingdom would be torn from Saul and given to another. An insight into what God deemed important is indicated by Samuel's profound words, "Obedience is better than sacrifice" (1 Sam. 15:22, NEB). Saul must have gotten the point, because he realized his fault and begged both Samuel's and God's forgiveness, confessing that his fear of the people caused him to allow their taking of spoils. Saul was genuine in his sorrow for his sins but it seemed too late—too many wrongs had been committed and his destiny appeared determined. The two parted and never met again.

It was now time for God to reveal to Samuel the identity of the man who should replace Saul as king. Although he was fearful for his life, Samuel, being directed by God, went to the house of Jesse and sought out David, his youngest son. As David was anointed in the presence of his family, the Spirit of the Lord came upon him as it had come upon Saul. The difference for David was that the Spirit would be with him from that day forward.

By this time the Spirit had left Saul and an evil spirit had taken its place. Because of the bad mood which accompanied the evil spirit, it was suggested by one of Saul's servants that a musician be employed who could play the harp and thus soothe away his bad mental state. This plan brought Saul and David together for the first time, and David entered Saul's service not only as private harpist but later as his armor bearer.

It was while fighting their old enemy, the Philistines, that the giant Goliath stood before the Israelite army, challenging any Hebrew to come out and fight him. Although young and without any military experience, David nevertheless killed the giant, drawing upon skills learned earlier while protecting his father's sheep from wild animals. This heroic deed was the beginning of David's ascent toward the throne and

also the beginning of Saul's downward path to disgrace
and ruin. The rout of the Philistines was heralded by
the people during the army's homecoming, with songs
and dances. One of the refrains spoke of "Saul killed
thousands but David killed tens of thousands" (1 Sam.
21:11, author's translation). For a man in Saul's frame
of mind, this had to be a great humiliation. From that
point on he kept a jealous eye on David. He probably
would have taken action against him if he had known
that David was already God's choice as successor to the
throne.

It began to dawn on Saul that God's Spirit had
truly departed from him and was now with David. This
became evident one night while David was playing the
harp. Saul flew into a rage and made two unsuccessful
attempts to pin him to the wall with a spear. More and
more David pleased the people, the army officers, and
even Saul's family, but at the same time raised in the
king greater and greater distrust for everybody. One
plan to get David killed was to promise his daughter
Michal in marriage if David would provide a bride price
of one hundred Philistine foreskins. Saul was sure that
that kind of activity would undoubtedly expose him to
mortal danger. Eager to fulfill his part of the bargain,
David and his men went out and killed Philistines. To
be doubly sure, they killed enough to provide twice as
many foreskins as specified. These were counted out
before the king and he, in turn, gave Michal to be

David's wife.

Saul had become deranged with feelings of hatred and jealousy to the extent that he sought David's life more intensely than he fought against the Philistines. David spent his days successfully beating the Philistines and, at the same time, keeping a step ahead of Saul. One day some priests befriended David and his men and even consulted God on their behalf. When Saul, who now believed almost everyone to be a traitor, heard this he had the eighty-five priests murdered and their town leveled.

On a number of occasions David had ample opportunity to take Saul's life but would not because of his regard for the fact that Saul had been anointed king by God's representative. David tried over and over to prove that he was not the king's enemy, but Saul's twisted mind refused to believe it. At times Saul seemed to admit his wrong but then would suddenly change and be obsessed with destroying David.

In order to take advantage of the civil strife between David and Saul the Philistines once more mustered their forces for an attack on the Israelites. Fear took hold of Saul and he once again asked God for direction. As before, there was no answer. In desperation he sought out a witch who might be able to contact the spirit of Samuel, who had died years before. A woman of Endor obliged him, and the specter of Samuel appeared. Saul asked what he should do about the upcoming battle. Samuel answered that because of Saul's disobedience, the Israelites would lose the battle and he and three of his sons would perish. The following days saw the predicted defeat. Jonathan and his two brothers were killed. Saul was wounded by archers and, fearing that he might be captured alive, ordered his armor bearer to end his life. Upon being refused, Saul fell on his own sword in suicide. Their leader gone, the Israelites fled and the victors took over and occupied the disputed territory.

From a human perspective, Saul seemed at first to be an excellent choice to lead the nation. He was a humble man. He was attractive and therefore had great popular appeal. Although God was reluctant to give the Hebrew nation a human king, he did choose Saul, and he gave him the spiritual preparation for the work. With such a great beginning, what went wrong?

The bad conduct of Saul can be traced to at least two basic flaws in his personality. First, when left to himself, he had difficulty making wise decisions. What he lacked was the vision and the patience to contemplate the far-reaching results of a particular act or deed. Usurping Samuel's priestly authority and the rash prohibition on eating are but two examples of this kind of shortsightedness. The second prominent weakness in Saul was his inability to accept a situation or person which might in any way appear competitive with his own interests. It began with the conflict over

Samuel's authority as spiritual leader and was later carried over into his relationship with David. It seems that this may have caused the deep emotional damage which rendered him a mental wreck during the later years of his reign.

Very very few of us can identify with the leadership responsibility thrust upon the somewhat unwilling first king of this beleaguered nation. Saul was a brave warrior and did fulfill, in a military capacity, the protective expectations of his supporters. The other half of what the new nation so desperately needed, the spiritual dimension, never showed itself in spite of God's initial blessing and Samuel's continued assistance. In their eagerness to have a king the people opposed God's will and therefore were not totally blameless of what befell them when Saul's end came.

The story of Saul is terribly sad. The potential for grand leadership appeared at the outset, but the fundamental weaknesses of poor judgment and pride of the man chosen as Israel's first king resulted in failure and death for the man and near defeat for the nation.

# 3
# Absalom

## The Backfiring of a Betrayal

The deaths of Saul and Jonathan were very difficult for David to accept personally, even though it brought to an end the fugitive life forced upon him by Saul's relentless pursuit.

David, who had been privately anointed king by Samuel many years earlier, now sought God's instructions as to the next steps he should take. He was directed to move to Hebron, a city of Judah. It was here that David was made king over the house of Judah and he reigned for seven and a half years. During this period, there was fierce fighting between the house of David and the house of Saul, but the balance of power gradually shifted in favor of David. After much conflict and many deaths on both sides, the people of Benjamin and the other ten tribes finally pledged allegiance to David and, for the first time, the nation was united. This, then, was the beginning of a golden age during which the nation became prosperous and strong. Under one supreme leader the nation's capital was moved to Jerusalem, and from there David ruled the Hebrew people for the next thirty-three years.

During this period, David was successful in defeating his country's long-standing enemies, the Philistines, forcing them out of the area that they had overrun during the time of Saul. The extent of the territory held by the twelve tribes was now all the land of Canaan which had been promised to Abraham. David accomplished strong consolidation of the tribes, both politically and spiritually. David's problems for the next few years were to come not from external enemies but from within his family and private life. It began with the adulterous relationship between David and Bathsheba which he tried unsuccessfully to cover up by having her husband killed. Before the birth of their firstborn, David took Bathsheba as his wife. God's judgment of David's crime was that violence would occur within his own family and that the child conceived in the affair would die. The second part of the punishment was carried out shortly after the baby was born. The first part would occur later and involve another of David's sons. Bathsheba bore him three more sons, the most notable being Solomon.

While living in Hebron, each of David's six other wives had given him a son. The oldest, and apparent heir to the throne, was Amnon, the next was Chileab, and the third son was Absalom. It was Absalom who caused his father great pain and anguish as the person whose treachery would complete David's earthly penalty for his sin with Bathsheba.

The story begins when Amnon fell in love with his half-sister Tamar, who was a full-sister to Absalom. Amnon appeared so distressed that his cousin Jonadab inquired as to the trouble. Amnon explained that he did not have the courage to approach Tamar to express his feelings. To help solve Amnon's problem, his cousin suggested that Amnon pretend to be sick enough to be confined to his bed, and that he request that Tamar come to his bedside, prepare a meal, and serve it to him. David was unaware of the motive and, believing it to be a reasonable request, directed that Tamar indulge Amnon while he was "sick." The girl went to Amnon's bedroom and prepared a meal, but when she offered the food to him, he refused it and ordered all but Tamar from the room. Again pretending to want the food, he got within reach of her, grabbed her, and told her to get into his bed. She pleaded with him not to dishonor her but he disregarded her strong objections, over-powered, and raped her. Moments after fulfilling his long-anticipated desire, his strong love turned to a stronger hatred, and in disgust he ordered her out of his bed and out of the room.

When Absalom learned that his sister Tamar had been violated by Amnon, he said neither an unfriendly nor a friendly word to him but only tried to comfort his sister. David's reaction was that of anger, but he took no action of discipline against Amnon because he was the eldest and much loved by his father. The absence of any punishment for such a dreadful crime against his sister must have deepened Absalom's abhorrence of his half-brother.

Two years later Absalom asked his father David if the entire royal family might gather at his home for a sheepshearing festival. David refused the invitation himself but did allow all of his sons, the princes, to attend. Absalom's real plan was revealed to his servants with instructions that they should wait until after the feast when Amnon had enough wine and upon a prearranged signal fall upon him and kill him. When the fatal blows were struck, the other princes scattered and hastily rode home.

A rumor reached David that Absalom had murdered all of the princes. Believing this false report, he and his servants tore their clothes and threw themselves to the ground in unbearable grief. It was Jonadab who corrected the error, explaining that only Amnon was dead, revenged by Absalom for the ravishment of his sister. Just then the princes arrived with the details that in truth Amnon had been slain and also that Absalom had fled the country.

For three years Absalom lived in exile with his grandfather Talmai, the king of Geshur, a small country in Syria. By now David became reconciled to the death of Amnon and was beginning to desire Absalom's return home. It was Joab, David's commander of the armed forces of the kingdom, who was instrumental in persuading David to recall Absalom and restore him to the royal family. Given permission, Joab went to Geshur and returned with Absalom to Jerusalem. David still was not ready for a complete reconciliation and continued to refuse a face-to-face meeting for two more years. Finally, with Joab again as intermediary, the father and son were reunited.

Once home again Absalom began a very serious campaign to gather support from the people for his bid to become successor to his aging father. Absalom's personal appeal was enhanced by the fact that he was a very handsome man and was known to have had no blemishes from his head to his feet. He seems to have had luxuriant hair that was admired for its fullness. One of his ploys was to intercept persons who were seeking David's judgment on a matter and imply that they might not get a hearing from the king, but that if he were in charge, everybody would receive fair and just treatment. In this way he sought to win people over to support his campaign to become king. After four years of preparation, the time seemed right for Absalom to make his move.

To arouse no suspicions in his father, Absalom asked if he might go to Hebron in order to fulfill a religious vow he had made while in exile. The purpose

was very appealing to David, since Hebron was the
burial ground of the patriarchs and also the former
capital city where he had been proclaimed king.
Absalom was granted permission because he knew by
now just what an indulgent father wanted to hear from
his son.

Once on the road to Hebron, the conspiracy began
to gain momentum. Even some of David's close com-
rades joined forces with Absalom. A particularly
disappointing defection was that of David's chief coun-
selor Ahithophel. So fearful of the possibility that this
man's great wisdom might now be turned against him,
David prayed that God would defeat any counsel given
to Absalom by Ahithophel.

The invasion of Jerusalem by Absalom's army was
imminent. David believed that if he and his family and
supporters were to remain, it would mean certain
death for all. Ten of David's concubines were left in
charge of the palace and a hastily formed spy network
was established. The retreat to the countryside was a
sad spectacle, with the old king bareheaded and bare-
foot once again running for his life. The procession
moved out of the city and did not stop to rest until it
reached the Jordan River.

David had given instructions to a friend, Hushai,
to return to the palace when Absalom took over the city
and claim that he was switching loyalties from David to

the new king. Zadok the priest, who also stayed, would pass any important information from Hushai on to his son Ahimaaz and on to David.

Meeting with little resistance, Absalom and his company invaded and took Jerusalem. Absalom along with Ahithophel and Hushai began to make plans for follow-up strategy to complete the takeover of the kingdom. The first piece of advice Ahithophel gave Absalom was that he should prove his resoluteness concerning his desire to be king by publicly violating his father's harem. Absalom agreed and proceeded with plans for his first public act as would-be king. A portion of the roof on top of the palace was prepared and there, in full view of the people, Absalom had intercourse with David's concubines.

Ahithophel next advised Absalom to allow him to immediately take men and pursue David with the intent of killing only the king, because without their king, the people would be easily brought to Absalom's side. This plan pleased Absalom, but desiring a second opinion, he asked Hushai for his advice. Now Hushai knew that Ahithophel's plan to surprise David would probably work, since the king would not have had time to get organized after such a chaotic retreat. His answer, then, was that David and his fighting men were fierce and cunning and that Ahithophel's suggestion would not work. He went on to advise that they should wait until Absalom's popular support had reached a

high level at which time the entire nation led by
Absalom himself, could go out in search of David and
annihilate him and all his family. Hushai's advice was
bad from a military standpoint but, because it was very
appealing to Absalom's ego, it won the day. Ahithophel
knew that following this second plan would doom
Absalom's kingly aspirations, and so he went to his
hometown, set his house in order, and hanged himself.

The spy system functioned well, and David was
kept informed of all that went on at the palace. The day
came when Absalom and his men took the field against
David, but by this time King David was sufficiently
organized, having been provided with food and sup-
plies by local civilian supporters. Because his men
persuaded the king not to lead the battle personally,
David organized the people into three groups and
appointed a commander to head each group. David's
final order to his officers, in the hearing of the whole
army, was that they should spare Absalom and deal
gently with him.

The battle ensued and David's forces routed the
enemy. Most of the fighting took place in a very thick
forest, which resulted in more troops being killed by
the forest than by the sword. Absalom was one of those
who fell victim to the forest. While riding beneath an
oak, his head with its magnificent hair was caught in
the branches and his mount continued on, leaving him
suspended from the tree. Joab, one of the three

commanders, was brought word of Absalom's plight. After chiding the messenger for not killing Absalom on the spot where he found him, Joab rode to the oak tree and promptly stabbed the helpless Absalom in the chest with three sharp instruments, darts or stakes. Joab's armor bearers finished him off, threw his body into a pit, and covered it with a huge pile of rocks. With the leader dead, the battle was over and the struggle for the throne ended.

Violent men often die in violent ways, and Absalom's death seemed to follow that pattern. But for him there was the added irony that the very hair that was central to his external personal attractiveness, which probably misled many to confuse personality with character, became part of the snare of his deathtrap. Even in burial, there was no hint of respect or dignity; a makeshift tomb of a nearby ditch and heap of field stones made up his final place of unrest.

The death of his son was such a shocking blow to David that he mourned to the exclusion of all thoughts of celebrating his enemy's defeat or of congratulating the men who fought the victorious battle. His mood so pervaded the whole army that upon their return they entered the city like men who had lost rather than won the war. It was Joab who pointed out to David that in spite of his personal grief over the loss of his son, he must consider his role as restored king and acknowledge his appreciation to the people.

It is very difficult to find any redeeming features in Absalom's life. Although one might see a degree of caring in his concern for his sister's calamity, the premeditated murder of her attacker seems to be the more accurate indicator of his true character. Anyone who is able to nurse a murderous grudge for two whole years is probably ripe for almost any number of evil acts.

Absalom was certainly an opportunist. It cannot be overlooked that his vengeful murder of Amnon paved the way for his eventual claim to the throne by eliminating David's eldest son from the competition. He took advantage of the king repeatedly by exploiting David's naive and trusting perception of his sons. He was a traitor whose consuming ambition to be king brought him to the point of attempting to kill his own father.

As in the case of Esau many years earlier, once again we see the sovereign nature of God combine mysteriously with the human nature of a man to bring about profound events in the life of a family. Absalom's method of achieving his goals was based on deceit and ambition coupled with an ever present capability for violence. That all of this was directed toward his immediate family reveals the terrible picture of one who was coldly unmoved by even the closest of family relationships.

As one thinks about the evil in both Saul and

Absalom that was directed toward David, and then considers David's responses, it is not difficult to understand why God should designate him as "a man after [My] own heart" (1 Sam. 13:14) and promise that the second king of Israel would head a dynasty which would never end. David made many mistakes, but his reaction toward his sins was invariably the same—he confessed them and sought God's forgiveness.

# 4
# Ahab and Jezebel

## The Food for the Dogs

After the revolt by Absalom and his followers had been put down, it was difficult to reconstruct the badly divided nation. The civil war had weakened the monarchy and this tempted Sheba, another would-be leader, to take the throne. Joab again was the hero, and the rebellion was subdued. There followed more conflicts with the Philistines, and during one of these King David, now very old, was taken prisoner. Only a timely rescue by one of David's brave men prevented the king from being killed. After this episode, it was decided that he should never again go out to the battlefield.

David was near death, and it was time for one of his sons to be chosen king. Amnon had been murdered and the second son, Chileab, was probably dead. When Absalom was eliminated, the fourth son of David, Adonijah, was assumed to be the heir apparent. Among his supporters were Joab, David's commander, and Abiathar, one of the two high priests. All things pointed to Adonijah becoming king until Bathsheba reminded David he had promised that her son Solomon would succeed him. Urged by Bathsheba that immediate action must be taken to prevent Adonijah from ascending to the throne, David ordered Zadok the priest and Nathan the prophet to anoint Solomon and to publicly proclaim him king. This was accomplished that very day, and in David's presence King Solomon seated himself upon the throne. Adonijah and his followers ceased their plans, and all became supportive of the new king. It seemed as though all was going well until Adonijah pressed his luck too far by asking to marry the young nurse who had cared for David during his last days, and Solomon had him killed. This seemed to touch off a systematic purge of all who were in support of Adonijah. Solomon had Benaiah kill Joab and gave him Joab's position as commander of the army, and he removed Abiathar the priest and sent him into exile.

The nation thrived under Solomon's leadership, and during most of his reign there was peace and prosperity. He built the Temple in Jerusalem. He expanded geographically and economically national interests to a level unrivaled by any other country. The promises made to the Israelite forefathers seemed almost realized during this period. It probably was better than it had ever been, but, as we shall see, the condition of the nation was about to get worse.

Solomon's wisdom and the magnificence of his

kingdom were renowned. His success in dealing with other nations was in part due to marriage liaisons with the royal families of those countries. But this in turn brought a great deal of pagan religion into the king's own family, and this ultimately led to the decline and downfall of the great Hebrew nation.

The kingdom under Saul, David, and Solomon was now 120 years old. Each king had reigned about forty years. The idolatry which Saul and David had been partially successful in checking now began to become widespread through the country. Because King Solomon had embraced many pagan ways, God revealed to him that the kingdom was to be taken from him. God then raised up Jeroboam, the son of a member of Solomon's court, as the leader who would be given the ten-tribe portion of the nation which would be taken from Solomon's son. One day Jeroboam was traveling near Jerusalem when a prophet of God met him and explained that he had been chosen to be king over the ten northern tribes. He was told that the two southern tribes would continue to exist for the sake of David to preserve the dynasty in Jerusalem. Jeroboam now became King Solomon's major competition and the king sought to kill him, but he escaped to Egypt and remained there until Solomon's death.

The final division occurred when Solomon's son Rehoboam, who was about to assume leadership over the entire nation, sternly gave notice that his regime would be harder on the people than his father's. He came to this conclusion after consulting first with the older men who had counseled Solomon, and then with the men his own age. Unfortunately, he followed the advice of the latter, and the majority of the people rejected him as king. The time was right for Jeroboam to return and fulfill the prophecy. From this point on, the ten northern tribes would be known as Israel and the Southern Kingdom composed of Judah and Benjamin would be called Judah.

Jeroboam became the first king of Israel and one of his early official acts was to introduce calf worship into his nation's religious life. He did this not because he personally adhered to this Egyptian import, but because he believed the people needed a substitute for the true God lest they return to Rehoboam. Calf worship became so deeply implanted during Jeroboam's reign that it lasted until the nation was taken into captivity two hundred years later.

The relationship between Israel and Judah for the next two centuries was marked with frequent and bitter conflicts. In addition to civil strife, each had problems from the intruding nations of Egypt and Syria. The quality of the kings who ruled Judah averaged somewhere between poor and fair. They had their ups and downs spiritually, but nevertheless were able to maintain the Davidic dynasty through a line of twenty different leaders. This kingdom lasted 120 years longer than the Northern Kingdom.

Jeroboam and the eighteen kings of Israel who followed him were so bad that one wonders how this branch of the Jewish nation lasted as long as it did. Idolatry and its accompanying evil practices were a way of life for both king and people. It is in this setting that we find our next villain.

Probably the worst time in Israel's history was the twenty-two years during which Ahab was king. He was the seventh king and entered the office over fifty years after Solomon's death. He inherited the throne from his father Omri who during his reign had moved the capital of the Northern Kingdom from Tirzah to a city that he built and named Samaria. It was here that King Ahab and his wife Jezebel ruled the land.

Ignoring God's specific warning against taking a wife of another nation, Ahab had selected Jezebel, the daughter of Ethbaal, king of Sidon. Ahab seems to have made the same mistake Solomon made, and the results were as tragic. From her idolatrous Phoenician homeland, she brought the religion of Baalism and had a temple built in Samaria for the worship of the god Baal. The worship included the sacrifice-killing of children by their own parents. The king and queen were patrons of 400 Baal priests at the temple in Samaria.

Elijah was a prophet who played a very important

role in the lives of Ahab and Jezebel. He seems to have been sent by God expressly to frustrate the efforts of those who propagated Baalism. The first recorded encounter between Ahab and the prophet was the occasion of his terse announcement to the king that there would be a long drought which would not end until Elijah himself gave the word. Having given Ahab that bad news, Elijah promptly left Samaria and went into hiding.

Three years later Elijah was told by God to again contact Ahab. By now the famine was so bad that the king himself, accompanied by Obadiah, the governor of his household, went to search for any remaining grassland that would keep his cattle from starving. The man Obadiah was a secret worshiper of the Lord, for when Jezebel had tried to exterminate all of the prophets of God, he was able to preserve a band of one hundred men by hiding them and providing them with food. Ahab and Obadiah decided to go in different directions to expedite the search. It was Obadiah who met Elijah and brought him to Ahab.

Elijah proposed a simple contest in which he, the only prophet of God left in Israel, and some four hundred and fifty prophets of Baal, plus four hundred prophets of the goddess Asherah (Ashtaroth) would gather at Mount Carmel and before all the people settle the question as to who was the true God. A bull sacrifice was prepared and laid upon an altar. The prophets of Baal spent most of the day praying to their god to send fire to burn the offering. They ranted, raved, and even cut themselves with knives in order to get their god's attention, but nothing happened. Now it was Elijah's turn. He built an altar made of twelve stones—one for each of the tribes. He prepared the sacrifice and the wood, and to make sure that the final outcome would be most impressive, had the altar and everything around it soaked with water three times. Elijah then prayed a short, simple prayer to God that he vindicate himself and Elijah for the people's sake. Suddenly the fire fell! It consumed not only the wood and the offering but also the water and even the stones. The people fell to their knees, acknowledging and praising God. Elijah and the people then took all of the Baal prophets down from the mountain and executed them. Elijah's parting word for Ahab was that he go home and wait for the oncoming rain that would signal the end of the drought.

Understandably, Jezebel was furious when told of the demise of the entire Baal priesthood. She immediately dispatched a message to Elijah that she was going to kill him by the following day. The threat was effective, for it caused him to run for his life, wandering alone in the desert for more than a month.

Back in Samaria, Ahab was having great difficulty with Ben-hadad II, king of Aram, who was threatening to invade the capital city. A prophet of God assured

Ahab that he would be victorious if he would personally lead a surprise attack. Ahab immediately went into the nearby hills with his army of over two hundred soldiers plus seven thousand citizen militia and defeated the forces which had laid siege to the city. Ben-hadad escaped and regrouped for another attack. Once more Ben-hadad prepared for the battle, but this time he planned that the engagement should take place on the plains, because it was thought that the God of Israel was a hill god and could only be effective there. After seven days of stalemate, the battle finally took place, and within one day Ahab's army routed the Aramaeans for a second time. This time Ben-hadad was captured, but his life was spared because he promised to restore cities which had previously been taken from Ahab's father, Omri, by Ben-hadad's father, Ben-hadad I. Another prophet, pretending to be a soldier who had failed to properly guard a prisoner, got King Ahab to declare that a fighting man guilty of that kind of negligence deserved death. The prophet then removed his disguise and announced that the king had pronounced sentence upon himself because he had "lost his prisoner" (1 King 20:40, author's translation), the king of Aram. The resulting condemnation foretold that Ahab would forfeit his life for Ben-hadad's life. The king went home to Samaria so disturbed by this latest encounter with one of God's messengers that he found no pleasure in the day's successful military action.

There was a man named Naboth who owned a vineyard near the palace at Samaria. One day Ahab went to Naboth and offered to buy the land outright or to exchange it for a superior vineyard at another location. Naboth was unwilling to sell or trade because the land had been in his family for many years. Ahab was so disappointed that he went home, went to bed, and refused to eat. When Jezebel found out from her husband what was bothering him, she told him not to worry, for she would make him a gift of the land. She proceeded to arrange for Naboth's death by having him falsely accused of cursing God and the king. The elders of Naboth's hometown of Jezreel carried out the details and Naboth was promptly stoned to death outside the city walls.

Upon hearing the news that Naboth was dead, Ahab was so delighted that he jumped out of bed and ran to look at his newly acquired property. During Ahab's stroll through the vineyard, Elijah showed up with another message of bad news from God. The grisly prophecy declared that dogs would lick up Ahab's blood where the dogs had licked up Naboth's, and that the dynasty begun with Omri would be cut off. In addition, because of Jezebel's part in the affair and because of her bad influence upon Ahab, she was condemned to die and her body would be eaten by dogs near the city wall of Jezreel. At this Ahab was overwhelmed by guilt and expressed genuine repentance for his sin. Due to Ahab's temporary change of heart, these disasters were postponed until after his death.

The next three years were peaceful. In fact, there were such good relations between Israel and Judah that their respective kings, Ahab and Jehoshaphat, decided upon a cooperative venture of taking back the city of Ramoth-Gilead which had been conquered previously by the Aramaeans under Ben-hadad. Jehoshaphat, who was probably the more spiritual of the two, asked that God be consulted about the undertaking. All four hundred of the prophets on hand in Ahab's court claimed that the attack should take place and that God would deliver the victory. Suspicious that Ahab's prophets might be giving desired rather than wise counsel, Jehoshaphat sought a second opinion. Ahab hesitantly admitted that there was another prophet, Micaiah, available, but that in the past his pronouncements had always been bad about anything concerning the king.

When brought before the two leaders and asked his opinion about attacking Ramoth-Gilead, Micaiah facetiously parroted what the other prophets had said. Although what Micaiah said was what Ahab wanted to hear, he was so accustomed to the prophet giving what Ahab thought to be contrary advice that he demanded that Micaiah tell the truth this time. Micaiah immediately obliged the king, reversed himself and predicted that during the battle, the men of Israel would be scattered like sheep with no shepherd, and that God's plan was to get Ahab into the battle by sending him bad advice through his lying prophets. At this the prophet was thrown into jail and the two kings marched off toward Ramoth-Gilead.

As they went into combat, Ahab hid his identity by not wearing his royal garb but nevertheless suggested that Jehoshaphat appear in his usual apparel. The strategy of Ben-hadad was to concentrate all efforts upon engaging only King Ahab in battle. When sighting Jehoshaphat, whose appearance was that of a king, they mounted an attack, but did not continue upon discovering that he was not Ahab. In spite of his efforts to protect himself Ahab was hit and seriously injured by an arrow which someone had randomly shot during the fray, and by the day's end the king had died of his wound. That evening when Ahab's chariot in which he had died was being cleaned, the dogs licked up his blood, thus partially fulfilling Elijah's words spoken in Naboth's vineyard.

After Ahab's death, his older son Ahaziah became king. But after less than two years he died as the result of a fall. Ahab's younger son Jehoram succeeded his brother and reigned for twelve years. He lost his life at the hands of Jehu, a man who had been commissioned by God to punish the house of Ahab. It was the postponed curse upon Ahab's family that was fulfilled when

Jehu shot Jehoram through the heart with an arrow and threw his body into the very pit where Naboth had died of the stoning at Jezreel. And it was Jehu who also had Jezebel thrown from a window to her death, but before she could be buried the dogs had eaten most of her remains.

The Bible states that there was no man like Ahab, who had sold himself to sin, and that Jezebel was the cause. Ahab's bad conduct, although often prompted by his unscrupulous wife, seems to be primarily due to weakness of character. When presented with the decision of marriage to a non-Israelite, he was weak to both the person of Jezebel and to the prospect of politically advantageous ties with another nation. Once married, he allowed not only the spread of Baalism but also the systematic annihilation of almost all vestiges of the worship of the true God. Even in the face of the dramatic show of God's hand at Mount Carmel, he seemed powerless to effect any change in his behavior.

His lack of self-discipline accounted for his failure to take Ben-hadad's life during the second campaign against the Aramaeans. This is reminiscent of Saul's dealing with Agag, the king of the Amalekites. Ahab's error came back to haunt him years later during the third campaign, when the very one he had foolishly spared earlier commanded the opposing force encountered in his last battle.

The events surrounding Ahab taking Naboth's

vineyard display vividly his almost childish inability to accept or respect the rights of another. Faced with Naboth's refusal to sell, a truly strong king would have gone ahead and taken the land outright, but Ahab went into his bedroom and pouted because he could not have what belonged to someone else. Even after being reminded that he was king and should act like one, he still needed the forceful hand of Jezebel to get the job done.

As a reasonably good military leader, it would seem appropriate that his end come during some heroic encounter in which death would occur amid the full glory of his role as soldier-king, but this was not the case. Ahab, in a final show of cowardly weakness, went to battle denying his identity as king and was mortally wounded because of the fortuitous flight of an arrow haphazardly shot by some unknown bowman.

# 5
# Haman

## The Hanging on His Own Gallows

The kingdoms of Israel and Judah existed side by side for about one hundred and thirty years after Ahab's death, sometimes engaged in war against one another and at other times fighting common foes. It was under Hoshea, the nineteenth king of the ninth dynasty, that Israel, the Northern Kingdom, was finally overrun by the Assyrians. Samaria, the capital, was conquered and any who survived were captured and transported to Assyria as slaves. It was the Assyrian's practice to exile conquered peoples and then colonize the land. This technique was a great deterrent to a nation's resurgence and also strengthened the victor's control over the frontiers of an expanding empire. Over a hundred years later Assyria fell to the Babylonians.

The Southern Kingdom, with its one dynasty and twenty kings, lasted another one hundred and thirty-five years. It was attacked a number of times over a period of twenty years by Nebuchadnezzar, king of the

Babylonian Empire. The conquest was ruthless and complete with destruction of Judah's capital city Jerusalem and the carrying away of thousands of the best of the nation's people. Zedekiah, the last king of Judah, was forced to watch his sons murdered, had his eyes put out, and was taken to Babylon where he died.

Among the educated and talented Jews who were taken captive to Babylon was Daniel, who eventually became famous for his wisdom and his ability to interpret dreams. He seems to have been in favor with King Nebuchadnezzar and later with Belshazzar. It was through Daniel and others like him that God was able to continue his plans for the Jewish nation even during its captivity. Daniel survived in the court of two major Babylonian kings and was retained in a similar position even after the fall of the empire. In fact, it was he who interpreted the famous writing on the wall which forecast the overthrow of Babylon by a coalition of the Medes and Persians. The very night the prophetic words appeared the invading armies took the great city and ended the seventy years of Babylonian domination in that part of the world.

The Persians now were in command. Because they emphasized the tribute-paying capacity of conquered people and also because of Daniel's influence upon Persia's King Cyrus, men like Ezra and Nehemiah were allowed to return to Judah and rebuild the capital city of Jerusalem.

An insight into the forces that caused the conquerors to sponsor the regathering of the Hebrews back in their homeland can be found in the story of Esther, the Jewish girl who became queen of Persia. It is within this episode which describes a people's fight for survival that we find Haman.

The story takes place in Susa, one of Persia's capital cities, as King Xerxes was about to embark upon an invasion of Greece. He, his military leaders, and government officials marked the occasion with extensive celebrations that lasted one hundred and eighty days. At the close of these festivities another group of guests, citizens of the city, were invited for a week of additional feasting and entertainment. The king showed off the furnishings of his palace and displayed his wealth while Vashti, the queen, entertained the women guests in the royal apartments in another part of the palace.

As more and more wine was consumed, the king, believing that the display of his beautiful wife would befit the occasion, sent for Vashti so that he could parade her in royal attire before the guests. His messengers went to the queen and returned with her flat refusal of the king's request. This angered Xerxes so much that he immediately consulted with his advisors as to how he should respond to this act of defiance. One of them pointed out that if Vashti went unpunished for her disobedience to her husband's command, women of the realm might think that they could do the same to their husbands. He further advised that Vashti be divorced, never again to appear with the king, and that another woman be made queen. This idea met with the king's approval and that very day Vashti was removed. The disposition of the problem was publicized throughout the royal provinces in all languages so that "men would not lose the control of their wives" (Esther 1:20, author's translation).

It became necessary to find a new queen and a search was set in motion with announcements going to all the provinces seeking candidates. The requirements included being young, virgin, and beautiful. The girls who qualified were to be brought to Susa where they would reside in the women's area of the palace to be prepared for their appearance before the king. The elaborate procedures for getting each girl ready for her turn with the king took twelve months.

One of those who went through this process was a Jewish girl named Esther. Her cousin Mordecai, an older man who had adopted her, was one of the many Jews who had been captured in Jerusalem and brought to this foreign land by Nebuchadnezzar. He belonged to the tribe of Benjamin. It was he who urged Esther to enter the competition, instructing her not to reveal her Jewish nationality. Esther was not only beautiful but also was very wise in taking the counsel of those who assisted her during the year of preparation. In fact, she was so liked and admired by all who knew her that it was no surprise that King Xerxes fell in love with her and chose her to be queen.

All during this time Mordecai had kept in close touch with Esther and in so doing was very knowledgeable about the affairs around the palace. One day he heard that two of the court eunuchs were planning to assassinate the king. He was able to get word to Esther and she, in turn, informed the king of the plot. The information was investigated, the two men were hanged, and the entire affair was recorded in the royal records crediting Mordecai for his part in alerting the king to the conspiracy.

Now there was a man named Haman who rose to a position second only to King Xerxes. He was a very ambitious person and was quite proud of having been recently promoted to this high post. As was the custom in those Persian circles, all persons of lower rank were supposed to bow down and do obeisance when in Haman's presence. Everyone in the palace and at court did as was expected except Mordecai the Jew. When this came to Haman's attention, he was infuriated. When he found out that Mordecai was a Jew, he decided not to try to confront him directly, but began to plot a means by which he might exterminate all of the Jews in Persia and thus rid himself of the only one who would show him no honor.

Haman proceeded with his plan, but because of

superstition, he cast lots in order to find out the best
time to carry out the mass killing of the Jews. Once the
date was set, he approached King Xerxes to get his
support for the project. He explained that there was a
race of people in their land who had strange rules and
customs, who did not keep the king's laws, and,
therefore, should be eliminated. As an added induce-
ment Haman promised to deposit a large sum of money
into the king's treasury. Xerxes seemed impressed
with Haman's idea and gave him full use of the royal
signet ring in order to carry out the details.

A written order then went out over the entire
country that on the prescribed day, all non-Jewish
citizens should kill all Jewish men, women, and children and take their possessions. Because they were an
alien people and numerically inferior to the Persian
populace, it loomed as a distinct possibility that their
race could be exterminated. There was great mourning
and distress among the Jews, many going without food
and wearing sackcloth instead of clothes. It was not
until Esther was informed of Mordecai's woeful appearance outside the palace gate that she became aware of
the terrible fate in store for the Jewish people.

It was Mordecai who insisted that Esther make an
attempt to approach her husband on behalf of all the
Jews, including herself. Esther was not sure that the
king would grant her an audience even though she was
queen. Everyone, including the queen, knew that to

enter the king's presence without being invited meant certain death. In spite of her fear Esther promised that she would bring the matter to the king's attention if Mordecai and all the Jews of Susa would fast for three days in preparation for the queen's upcoming meeting with Xerxes.

Three days later the queen stood at the accustomed spot where one waited for the king to signal that entrance into his presence was permitted. The king greeted her warmly, for he had not seen her for a month, and proceeded to eagerly seek out the reason for her visit. Not wanting to get directly into the real purpose, she asked simply that the king and Haman come that very day to a banquet which she had prepared. Wanting to please his queen, the king summoned Haman and together they went to Esther's banquet.

It was during the after-dinner wine that the king, obviously delighted with Esther's willingness to entertain him and his prime minister, again inquired as to what her desire might be, adding in kingly fashion the promise of "half his kingdom" if that was what she wanted. Again she avoided revealing the primary request by courteously asking that the king and Haman attend another banquet planned for the following day, adding that at this next meeting she would finally make known her specific wish.

Haman left with a feeling of great satisfaction that

he was included in the limited guest list of those attending the queen's banquet. As he left the palace his happiness turned to disgust and anger upon meeting Mordecai, the one man in the entire city who would not show any deference to either him or his high office. Although irate with this situation, he maintained his self-control and went to his home.

Upon arriving there he gathered his family and friends about him and detailed his wealth, his large family, and particularly the honor of his appointment to the second highest office in the land. Finally he told of attending that day's exclusive banquet given by Queen Esther and the prospect of another banquet the next day. The mood of the conversation abruptly changed as Haman recalled Mordecai's resolute refusal to honor him. In fact, Mordecai's behavior so disturbed him that in the light of this problem his riches and prestige meant nothing.

Even though the plan was underway for the extermination of Mordecai along with all of the Jews, his wife and their friends suggested that a seventy-five foot high gallows be constructed in Haman's front yard and that Haman get the king's permission to hang Mordecai prior to the banquet the following day. That way Haman could attend the dinner and enjoy himself fully. Haman agreed to the plan and set up the gallows that evening.

That night, back in the palace, the king was having

trouble getting to sleep. For something to do, he had a courtier read aloud from the records kept of daily activities around the palace. By chance, the reading covered the events surrounding Mordecai's part in thwarting the attempt on the king's life. The king inquired about what reward had come to the man Mordecai for his noble service and was informed that no special recognition had been granted. At that moment the king sighted someone entering the outer court and upon being informed that it was Haman, signaled that he be ushered into the king's presence.

It seemed natural to the king that his prime minister would be an appropriate consultant in the matter regarding Mordecai. Therefore, his opening question to Haman solicited suggestions concerning what should be done for a person whom the king desired to honor. Sincerely believing that the king's failure to reveal the name of the person was in fact a subtle hint that he was to be the recipient, Haman launched into a description of a grandiose plan which included dressing the person in royal robes, placing a crown upon his head, and parading him through the center of town riding upon the king's own horse. Haman also suggested that one of the king's most honorable men lead the horse and call out to the people along the way, "This is what the king does to show his appreciation to a man loyal to the crown."

Having described what must have been one of his

most cherished fantasies, Haman waited anxiously for his king to give someone the order that all of it be carried out to the letter. To Haman's utter amazement the king was talking about someone else to be so honored and, to add to Haman's shattering disappointment, it was to be Mordecai, the very person whom Haman was seeking permission to hang. The most devastating part must have been the assignment which fell to Haman that he was to manage the complete program, including the task of leading the horse and repeating over and over the announcement he had composed for himself but now was to direct toward Mordecai, his hated enemy. Fortunately for Haman, the conversation never got around to the real reason for his late night visit.

The next day Haman carried out the king's orders in every detail and when it was over he went home to lick his wounds of embarrassment. While he was recounting the activities of his humiliating experiences of that day, a messenger arrived with the reminder that he was due at the queen's banquet and he hurried back to the palace.

Once again the dining was over and the wine was poured. The king resumed his inquiry as to the queen's wishes and she finally explained the whole matter. She pleaded for herself and for her people, explaining the plan which was underway to eliminate all of the Jews in the realm. Upon the king's demand for the name of the man who would dare such a move against his queen, Esther pointed an accusing finger at Haman, who by this time was wide-eyed with disbelief that the queen herself was a member of the nation he planned to exterminate. He was further shaken by the revelation that Mordecai, the man whose death he sought, was Esther's cousin. The king was so beside himself with rage that he went from the room to the adjoining garden. Now Haman realized that his only possible hope of saving himself from imminent mortal punishment was to plead with Esther for his life. He moved toward the place where she was reclining on her couch, intending possibly to bow or kneel before her, but in his haste must have stumbled and fell headlong upon her. Once more a case of bad timing brought the king back to the banquet room, and finding Haman momentarily sprawled across his beloved Esther, he accused him of the crime of assaulting her before his very eyes. Even in Haman's last desperate attempt to save his life, he not only failed miserably, but completely sealed his doom by appearing to molest the king's wife. At that moment an attending servant told of the newly-constructed gallows over at Haman's house which had been built for Mordecai's execution. With no hesitation the enraged king ordered the obvious, and Haman was taken home and hanged.

The good qualities of Mordecai and his kinship with Esther led the king to appoint him as a replacement for Haman. It was Mordecai who, in his new role as prime minister, was able to circumvent the irrevocable order that on the appointed date the Jews would be killed. This was accomplished by sending out a second notice stating that when the fateful day came, all Jews could defend themselves and fight against any who might attack them. So effective was this effort that many Persians of the country professed to be Jews to avoid possible harm from those who were "defending" themselves. In the capital city, the Jews took the opportunity and killed eight hundred of their enemies including Haman's ten sons. Out in the provinces a total of seventy-five thousand Persians were slain; there is no record of even one Jew having been harmed.

Haman's life appears to be a tragedy of errors. Almost all of his problems and mistakes stemmed from his exaggerated opinion of himself. Anyone who suffers from this personality trait is like a blind person who without help when moving about is destined to crash into things. A preoccupation with one's importance simply prevents a normal awareness of the outside world. Haman probably got to his honored position through the usual channels, but when we encounter him we find a man who believed himself to be superior in ways not related to his being prime minister. He was so taken by this belief that one "little" person's passive denial of it seemingly disrupts his whole life such that he would go to any lengths to remove that person.

He was so driven by one man's refusal to give him what he considered proper respect that he went to the insane extreme of trying to get rid of a great number of human beings in order to get at that one man. For most mature people in positions of honor this would be a minor irritation or of no moment at all. Even the well-organized plan was not a speedy enough resolution of the problem; he rashly built the gallows and blundered into his inevitable destruction.

If he had been paying attention to the people and events around him, he might have learned that Esther was Jewish and that her cousin Mordecai had done the king an important service. If his oversized ego had not gotten in the way he would not have presumed that the king was planning something special for him. A person with Haman's problem does not have room in his thinking for the possible good fortune of others but only thinks "me first" thoughts.

It is ironic, though, that Haman never did complete any of his murderous schemes except as they backfired upon him, his house, and his countrymen. He had all the necessary power and almost unlimited authority to carry out his plot, but his preoccupation with self and God's use of that weakness not only defeated his purposes completely but strengthened the Jews, making possible their return to the Promised Land.

# 6
# Herod the Great and His Son
## The Slaughter of Babies

The story of Haman is told in the last historical book of the Old Testament. From the time of Haman to our next bad character there was a period of over four hundred years, during which there is a very sketchy history of the Jewish people. We do know that some Jews returned to Palestine and were able to take up a fairly peaceful life in and around Jerusalem. Also during this extended period the exiles grew in number and prospered where they were in captivity. This larger portion of non-Palestinian Jews was known as the "Dispersion." Throughout all of their trials and tribulations it appears as though God was still caring for his people, but that his long-ago promise of a large nation established in a special geographical area was still quite remote.

It is important here to explain what is presently believed about the history and destiny of the Jews. Rather than employ theological labels which might involve extraneous issues, let us simply look at three of the most common views on this subject. The first of these claims that the promises made to Abraham and reiterated to his progeny are still to be fulfilled at a time when an independent state of Jewish origin is established in the Holy Land. Included in this is a yet-to-appear Messiah who will rule as a literal king and lead the nation politically and spiritually. For those who believe this to be correct, the events recorded in the New Testament, although occurring in the midst of Jewish history, are not highly significant. Another approach, somewhat like the first, holds that the promises should be interpreted literally and will be realized sometime in the future, but unlike it, that Jesus truly was the promised Messiah and that the present age is like a parentheses in time, during which non-Jews can become a part of the blessing of being God's people. A third opinion claims that the promises to the patriarchs are understood best if interpreted figuratively. It holds that God has turned away from the Hebrew nation as a whole because of its continued disobedience, that the true Jew is the individual who personally accepts Christ as Messiah, and that any significance inferred from agreements or covenants between God and Israel must logically apply to the Christian church.

As we discuss the following villains of the New Testament it is important to keep in mind that David's family line had not been broken during the almost silent years but that a small remnant continued to await rescue by God. The prophets had steadfastly maintained that in spite of captivity and suppression, the nation would survive and that a Savior descended from King David, of the tribe of Judah, would bring about the final triumph over all their enemies.

The Persian domination as a world power lasted until 332 BC. The era came to a close with the rise of the Greeks under Alexander the Great, who with his armies swept eastward and within five years had conquered all lands previously held by Egyptians, Assyrians, Babylonians, and Persians. Although these conquests included Palestine, the Jews seem to have been treated reasonably well by the Greeks. After Alexander the Great died, the extensive empire was divided among four of his generals. After some uncertainty as to which of the four regions should include Palestine, it came under the control of Egypt and remained there for the next one hundred years.

It was Antiochus III of Syria who in 198 BC invaded Palestine and took it from Egypt. His son, Antiochus IV, who followed him was so zealous to have the Jews of Palestine adopt Greek language and customs that his extreme efforts, among which was the desecration of the Jewish altar, led to the Maccabean revolt. This rebellion was successful and left the small Jewish nation relatively independent for the next hundred years. In 63 BC the Romans under Pompey invaded Palestine and, in order to maintain a firm hold on the conquered territory, set up a puppet government with Hyrcanus as high priest. Hyrcanus's organization of the territory under Roman domination placed Antipater as ruler over part of the area. Antipater was an Idumean, a descendant of Esau. This ancestry was probably in his favor from Rome's point of view for the person selected to govern such a deeply religious and nationalistic people.

Along the eastern edge of the Mediterranean Sea, the regions south to north were Idumea, Judaea, Samaria, and Galilee. The people of Judaea and Galilee were strong in the Jewish religion and traditions, while those of Idumea and Samaria were either diluted racially or had been forced to accept Jewish ways and, therefore, tended to welcome and generally cooperate with Roman rule.

As Antipater's influence widened, he procured for his oldest son Phasaelus the position of governor of Judaea, whose capital was at Jerusalem. He was also able to have his second son appointed governor of Galilee, and thus began the long and colorful political career of Herod I, who later came to be known as Herod the Great.

He first attracted Rome's attention by quelling a minor rebellion in the region of Galilee. He had pleased the Romans in neighboring Syria who had been victimized by these rebels, but because of his ruthless executions without trial of those who were captured he had angered the religious leaders in Jerusalem and they demanded that he be tried for the crime. Although they were a conquered people and under Roman rule, the Jews were allowed to carry on some religious and judicial activities. Since Hyrcanus was Herod's superior, it followed that he be tried by the Sanhedrin, a judicial council of seventy men. Ordered to appear, Herod went to Jerusalem and stood before the tribunal. He took with him a squad of soldiers and displayed such brash insolence which so intimidated the council that they voted overwhelmingly to acquit him. This was just the beginning of a long series of conflicts between the Jews and this arrogant, ambitious young man who would one day be their king.

Herod's power and influence grew over the next few years, but it took a war in Palestine with the Parthians, his own father's assassination, and the murder of Julius Caesar in Rome to set the stage for his ascendance to the throne.

The Roman world was shaken by the treasonous killing of the most famous of the Caesars in March of 44 BC. This event led to the leadership at Rome being shared by Antony and Octavian. Antipater, Herod's father, met his death through a poisoning arranged by Malichus, who feared the growing Rome-supported power the family was gaining. Herod himself avenged his father's death by killing Malichus. Herod and his brother Phasaelus now filled their father's position in the court of Hyrcanus and this brought more public exposure to the young governor. In 40 BC the Parthians, who had conquered Persia, invaded Palestine with the intention of pushing the Romans completely out of the area. In the face of what appeared to be his certain defeat, Herod fled the country. During his travels he was unable to get any assistance until he returned to Rome, where he persuaded Antony and Octavian that he should be appointed king of the Jewish state in Palestine.

Having been made king by the authority in Rome, he then proceeded back to Palestine to claim his throne. With only a small force of Roman soldiers, Herod reentered the country through the port at Acre in Galilee. Within two years, he had unseated the puppet government of the Parthians and for the next thirty-four years ruled as king, never wavering from his wholehearted loyalty to Rome.

Herod reigned in an atmosphere of political intrigue in a tenuous position over strongminded Jews who hated everything about him. His long tenure speaks well of his administrative skills. The price of keeping the upper hand in such a situation became very high indeed.

During his life as ruler of the Jews he had to keep a watchful eye on his own household as much as he did on his subjects. By his hand his enemies were summarily imprisoned, exiled, or assassinated. As the years went by the interest concerning which of his sons would succeed him caused the struggle to become more intense. During this stormy period Herod was responsible for the deaths of many of his family members including his second wife, her two sons, and the son of his first wife. This latter event occurred very late in the king's life and it is here that we meet him in the biblical narrative.

The king was now old and a life of hard living had left his body sick and broken and his temperament unpredictable. One day at his palace in Jerusalem a group of astrologers made inquiry as to the location of the birthplace of a child who would become King of the Jews. The expectation of a Messiah was widespread and was probably extant in the distant land from which these men had traveled. They had followed a moving star thus far and now believed their journey was near its end somewhere around Jerusalem. When Herod heard of this, he became very agitated and immediately consulted the Jewish priests as to where the Messiah was to be born. They answered that the writings of the prophet Micah foretold that it would take place in Bethlehem in Judah. He then held a private meeting with the visitors and after some interrogation, sent them on to Bethlehem with instructions to return and inform him of their finding the child so that he too might worship him. Because they were strangers, these men may not have understood Herod's murderous intentions. They continued to follow the star, and at the town of Bethlehem a few miles south of Jerusalem found the child Jesus with his mother Mary. After seeing the child they returned to their homeland but traveled an alternate route, being warned by God in a dream not to go back to Herod. At about this same time Joseph, Mary's husband, also was warned in a dream that he should take Mary and the baby to Egypt because Herod would soon come looking for the child to do away with this threat to his kingship.

When Herod finally realized that the astrologers had tricked him and were not going to return, he was so angry that he dispatched orders that all children under two years, living in or near Bethlehem, be killed. By the time this terrible act was committed, the little family was safe in Egypt and there they stayed until Herod died.

A few days prior to his death Herod changed his will, designating Archelaus, his fifth oldest son, as successor to the throne rather than Antipas, Archelaus's younger brother. The latter provision had been a part of his earlier will. At the time of his death there were at least three sons who appeared to be candidates, each with a claim to the throne. The matter was settled in Rome by Augustus Caesar, the former Octavian, who was now sole ruler of the empire. The compromise awarded the title of king to none of the claimants but did divide Palestine, giving rule of the northeast region to Philip, a seventh son, the region including Galilee to Antipas, and the southern portion comprised of Idumea, Judaea, and Samaria to Archelaus.

Again God spoke to Joseph in a dream and instructed him to return with his family to Israel. Upon entering the country he discovered that Archelaus had taken Herod's place in Judaea. Joseph knew of Archelaus's reputation and was afraid to settle in that part of the country under his rule. Once more in a dream God instructed Joseph, and he took his family back to the hometown of Nazareth in Galilee and lived there.

Herod the Great was more than a match for the brutal times in which he lived. His life appears to have been driven by strong forces of ambition and survival. Both of these traits can be used for good or evil, but this man built his life and career upon only the dark side of these characteristics. His ambition was to be achieved at any cost and, once achieved, he held onto his gains tenaciously, again at any cost.

It is not surprising that after many years of cruelty and violence against any who might stand in his way, the threat of an obscure child of a peasant family could trigger such a crime as the slaughter of many small children. By this time in his life, it was much more the paranoia surrounding his royal office than any real belief in the Scriptures that caused blind anger against the Christ child. His frame of mind must have dictated that anything or anybody who even remotely appeared to endanger his position would have to be swiftly and completely eliminated.

His lifelong fight with the Jews, which he realized late in life he might never win, prompted him to conceive a plan which would assure his being able to strike the last blow. As his death drew near he ordered that all the notable Jews be locked up in the hippodrome at Jericho and that at the moment he died, they all be executed. Knowing that the end of his miserable life on earth would give rise to nationwide celebrations, he believed he could turn the event into national mourning by the simultaneous deaths of most of the Jewish leadership. His plan ultimately failed, as those who were to kill the captives at Jericho let them go when Herod died.

Archelaus was as bad as his father Herod, but he lacked his father's skill and cunning in governing and was deposed ten years after assuming the position. This came about because of his cruel treatment of his subjects and his complete disregard for the Jewish laws and customs. An unlikely coalition of Jews and Samaritans complained to Augustus Caesar and, in addition, his brothers Philip and Antipas brought charges against him. All of this trouble resulted in his being banished, and his domain was reduced to the status of a province governed by Roman procurators. The original apportioning of Palestine among Herod's three sons had given Archelaus the best assignment because he was the oldest. Because Antipas received a lesser share of the area, he was awarded the dynastic title of Herod and came to be called Herod Antipas.

The reign of Herod Antipas was even longer than that of his father, Herod the Great. He seems to have inherited much of his father's ability to administer a hostile nation and at the same time maintain good relations with the leadership back at Rome. Augustus encouraged intermarriage across political and national lines, and therefore Antipas took as his wife the daughter of the Arabian king, Aretas IV. This move provided a friendly buffer at the eastern border.

A number of years later, Herod Antipas, while on a trip to Rome, visited his half-brother Philip. This was not the "Philip" who shared in the three-way division of the territory. Although even older than Archelaus, he seems not to have been interested in any public office at all. Philip had married his niece Herodias, whose father Aristobulus had been one of the victims of her grandfather, Herod the Great. During this visit, Herod Antipas fell in love with Herodias and she with him. When Herod Antipas returned home, he brought her along with the intention of disposing of his wife and marrying Herodias. Word of this unbelievable liaison reached Palestine and his wife before they did, and she escaped to the fort at Machaerus east of the Dead Sea and then went south to her father's home at Petra.

When the couple finally arrived, trouble at the eastern frontier had already erupted and Herod Antipas's father-in-law was beginning to take revenge for the mistreatment of his daughter and the breach in their political alliance. The marriage with Herodias that followed was particularly displeasing to the Jews because the Mosaic law specifically prohibited a man from marrying his brother's wife if the brother was still living.

There was a wilderness preacher named John who spoke out publicly against the king's immoral conduct. This so irritated the royal couple that they had John arrested and were holding him in the prison of the fort at Machaerus. John's ministry was prophesied as one which would pave the way for the work of Jesus of Nazareth. His activity was mainly preaching the coming kingdom and encouraging his listeners to repent and be baptized—thus the name John the Baptist. Herod Antipas was fearful that John might lead a religious rebellion if he were allowed his freedom but at the same time was afraid to put to death this most interesting and popular preacher.

It was on the occasion of the king's birthday, which was being celebrated at Machaerus, that the scheming Herodias was able to force the king's hand and silence John permanently. During the festivities of eating and drinking, the king requested that Salome, Herodias's daughter, dance before him and his guests. His step-daughter must have performed a very exciting dance, for it pleased him so much that he promised she could have anything that was in his power to give. It is not known whether or not the whole plot was worked out in advance, but when the girl asked her mother what request she should make Herodias was quick to suggest the gruesome gift of John's head on a dish, and Salome readily announced this to the king as the thing she desired.

Now the king was cornered. For a number of reasons he did not want to kill John, but because of the rash promise he had made with an oath before all of the party guests he ordered John beheaded and had the head delivered to the banquet room on a platter. This was presented to the girl and she gave it to her mother. This episode plus the broken treaty with Aretas caused domestic and foreign problems for Herod Antipas and Herodias the remaining eight years of their reign.

In AD 36, Aretas attacked and defeated Antipas's army so badly that the king had to seek Rome's help. By this time Tiberius had succeeded Augustus as emperor, and he responded to the call by dispatching the governor of Syria. This assistance to Palestine was delayed because of Tiberius's death until the Emperor Caligula could issue his orders concerning the matter. Because of the change of emperors, Herod Antipas was never able to take revenge against Aretas and two years later was banished, along with Herodias, to Gaul. A nephew, Agrippa I, was moving up the political ladder, and it was his accusations of treason against his uncle that determined Herod Antipas's final fate.

This Herod, much like his more famous father, was ruthless and cruel in his quest for power and gratification. His was a common problem in leaders who believe themselves to be above and exempt from the rules of society. His weakness concerning women shown first in the case of his brother's wife, and then in his response to the sensual dance of the beautiful Salome, seems to be the source of at least two far-reaching mistakes that contributed to his downfall.

Neither Ahab, Israel's worst king, nor Antipas, the next to the worst of the Herods, can be given all the "credit" for their evil behavior. The two most notoriously bad women of the Bible played major roles in the sin and downfall of these leaders. Both Jezebel and Herodius were loyal to and singularly ambitious for their men, but often in a twisted sort of way. Herodias's loyalty seems to have never changed; she stayed by the side of Herod Antipas during his political demise and permanent exile although this was not required of her.

Unlike his father, he appeared to have a slight personal interest in the evolving new religious ideas being presented by men like John the Baptist and Jesus of Nazareth. For a time after John's death, Herod

Antipas thought that Jesus was John resurrected from the grave, but was convinced otherwise when near the end of his reign he was called upon by Pontius Pilate to interview Jesus in the course of his trial.

So far the dynasty of the Herods had lasted close to seventy-five years. Herod the Great and his son, Herod Antipas, were both extreme in their evil methods of administering the affairs of state in Palestine. Although they were distantly related to the people they ruled, neither showed any understanding of the nation's special place in God's plan. Having ancestral ties to the patriarchs made their actions that much more repugnant to the Jewish populace. To be remembered most for the murder of a large number of little children and the senseless execution of John the Baptist, befits this father-and-son pair of villains who lived during the most significant time in religious history.

# 7
# Judas

## The Kiss of a Traitor

Except for the short stay at Bethlehem and Egypt in his infancy, Jesus lived his life under the rule of Herod Antipas. He, like his contemporary, John the Baptist, preached about the Kingdom. They spoke of a spiritual kingdom, which was difficult for Jews to understand who were expecting the Messiah to come as a king who would finally defeat all of their enemies and set up a literal kingdom.

Jesus began this ministry when he was thirty years old and the work lasted about three years. During this period, his travels were confined to a small geographical area along the Mediterranean Sea no more than seventy-five miles wide. He went as far north as Sidon, a city of Phoenicia, and as far south as Bethlehem. His ministry was inaugurated by his baptism at the hands of John the Baptist. This took place in the waters of the lower Jordan near the town of Bethany east of that river. After the forty days of temptation in the wilderness, he traveled up and down preaching, teaching, and healing. In these travels he attracted a small group of devoted men one, two, or three at a time, which became a fairly permanent body of twelve followers known as disciples. It is one of these disciples, Judas, who we now take up in our study of bad people.

The selection of these close companions had at least two practical advantages. Knowing that his death was an absolute necessity as a part of God's redemptive plan for his people, Jesus' teachings would have to be carried on by others after he was gone, and this could only be accomplished if he could give full-time intensive instructions to a relatively small group of students. Another reason was that he needed practical help in the organization to carry out routine day-to-day tasks such as preparing meals, securing lodging arrangements, and running errands. One of the more important assignments, which went to Judas, was the care of the little sack in which the group kept its money. Whether elected or appointed, Judas became the treasurer and probably was present when any financial transactions took place.

Jesus had a number of close friends which he often visited in the town of Bethany west of Jordan. Among these was a family of two sisters, Mary and Martha and their brother Lazarus. It was Lazarus whom Jesus had raised from the dead on an earlier occasion after the man had been in his grave for four days. On one of these visits a banquet was held in Jesus' honor and many people attended, including the disciples. Mary, one of the sisters, in order to show her devotion to the guest of honor, broke open a container of very expensive ointment-perfume and poured it on Jesus' feet, wiping away the excess with her long tresses. The fragrance was soon noted throughout the house and attention was drawn to its source.

It was Judas who, when he observed what was happening, inquired as to the reason for the purposeless waste of this very costly substance, commenting that selling it and giving the proceeds to poor people would be better than using it to bathe someone's feet. Judas saw here the likelihood of his being involved in the sale, and that some or all of the price would end up in the disciples' treasury and thus provide more that he would have access to for his frequent pilfering. He was correct in his estimate of the value of the perfume because this particular kind was scarce and had to be imported from faraway northern India.

Jesus came to Mary's defense with a mild rebuff to Judas by pointing out that their leader would be with them for only a short time while the poor would always be around. He went on to compliment Mary for her beautiful gesture and added an ominous note that she save the remaining amount of the liquid for his burial.

This allusion to his death was not premature. The chief Jewish leaders by now had had so many confrontations with Jesus that they were frantically looking for any means possible to do away with him. They knew that whatever scheme they hatched could not be carried out in public, because Jesus had won over the common people and had enormous popular support. It was finally Judas who stepped forward and provided the solution to their dilemma. He went to the chief priests and asked what amount they would be willing to pay him for his assistance in engineering Jesus' capture. The price was fixed at thirty silver coins. This amount was presented to Judas and from that time on he watched for the opportunity to perform his part of the contract.

It was now mid-April. Jesus and his twelve disciples were in Jerusalem at supper keeping the Passover feast, which was for Jews an annual commemoration of Israel's deliverance from Egypt more than thirteen centuries earlier. Jesus had tried again and again to hint of his upcoming death and its purpose, but the disciples never quite understood that their Messiah had to die in order that salvation could come to a lost world. Now as they fellowshipped around the table, Jesus became very bold and not only spoke plainly about his dying but also told them that one of their number would play the important role of traitor in assisting his enemies. Each man denied the charge but Jesus insisted that it was truly one of his companions at the table. He remarked that even though destiny demanded the evil deed, it would be better if the perpetrator had never been born.

As the meal progressed possibly amid conversation about the activities planned for the rest of the evening, including Jesus' usual walk and prayer in the secluded garden east of the city, Judas must have completed in his mind the details of his plan. As the supper ended Jesus spoke privately to him that he should go about his business and Judas left. No one seemed aware of any significance in Judas's sudden departure, assuming that as treasurer he had been sent to buy something or to make a gift to the poor.

Judas probably went directly to the priests and explained where Jesus would be during the evening and how he could be easily taken into custody. Later, with Judas in the lead, a small force of Temple police left the city and went straight to the garden where Jesus and some of his disciples had gone for prayer. For those who did not know Jesus on sight Judas had promised that he would single him out by greeting him with a kiss so that there would be no confusion as to whom they should capture. All went as planned. Jesus was bound and taken away and, as predicted earlier, all of his followers scattered into the night.

Now the Jews realized that they had to hold a trial in secret sometime that night. Otherwise, all of their efforts would be in vain if many people found out what was happening. Therefore, Jesus was taken directly to the high priest's house where the elders, chief priests, and doctors of the law had already assembled, even though it was against their laws to hold a night trial. Throughout the proceedings attempts were made to build a case against him but all these efforts failed. Finally, the high priest asked the crucial question whether or not Jesus was the Messiah. His unequivocal yes was more than enough to bring the assembly to a near unanimous agreement that he was guilty of blasphemy and that he should be put to death for that crime.

For the Jews the sentence of death was exactly what they wanted, but now they faced a new problem. Although according to Jewish law blasphemy was punishable with death by stoning, the Roman government would not allow them to carry out executions for any reason. The strategy now called for the Jews to make a political rather than a religious case against Jesus and get the Roman authorities to finish the work they had started. They secured Jesus in chains for the night and the next morning brought him to the governor, Pontius Pilate.

It is possible that Judas knew about Rome's prohibition of Jewish executions, and he may have believed that turning Jesus over to the Jews would never result in his being executed. But when morning came, and he observed that now the accusers were on their way to Pilate to get the sentence carried out, he was gripped with such remorse that the full impact of his role in the affair completely overwhelmed him. In one desperately hopeful moment he imagined that the return of the money he had been paid might in some way reverse the deed's effect. He went to the Temple and begged that they accept the return of the money, but when refused by the priests he cast the coins onto the floor and ran from the place. Despair and grief took control of his already shattered spirit and, believing that only in death could he find release, he went to a secluded spot and hanged himself.

At a gathering a number of weeks later Peter and the remaining disciples met to choose a replacement for the deceased Judas. Peter alluded to an Old Testament prophecy which foretold the fate of Jesus' betrayer, adding that at the time of death Judas had fallen to the ground with such force that his body burst open. Perhaps he hanged himself from some high place and the rope broke, resulting in the near unconscious body falling violently to the ground. This was the gruesome end of one of the most notorious traitors in all the Bible.

For over two years Judas and the other eleven disciples were probably the only persons who were truly close to Jesus, even closer than members of his own family. They witnessed firsthand the miraculous feeding of thousands, the healing of many sick and impaired individuals, and the exorcism of evil spirits. Judas certainly took an active part in the private discussions Jesus had with the group. Much of Jesus' encouragement, warning, and teaching was directed toward this intimate little band. Often the disciples would not quite comprehend the meaning of the Master's parable lessons, and later in private he would painstakingly reveal hidden truths which were meant especially for them. All of this Judas had as his store of knowledge and yet he betrayed the very source of these blessed experiences.

In the sketchy information we have about him, one difficulty which seems paramount was his problem with money. It was not just the surface interest in being able to have what money could buy, but a severe case of money love which so occupied his thoughts that consideration of more worthwhile things was excluded. Missing the profound significance of Mary's act of anointing Jesus' feet, but instead favoring selling the perfume, speaks clearly of his misguided interests. The crucial failing we finally see in Judas is his sale of his trusted position in the group for an amount of money equivalent to about a month's wages. If his motive had been political, then the money would not have entered the picture. If religious disagreement troubled him, all he had to do was simply walk away from the entire matter; Jesus invited people to believe in and follow him but never compelled them. Judas seems to have had money on his mind, for when a means appeared by which some could be acquired, he had no difficulty delivering his part of the bargain. It was not until the terrible consequences of his lust for money dawned upon him that he showed signs of remorse. But this realization must have unleashed all of the guilt stored in his soul over a lifetime of selling of self. His burden was too ponderously heavy to bear, and so he solved the problem by suicide. Later in the New Testament the apostle Paul points out that the love of money is the root of evil; but this admonition came too late for Judas, the man whose name has become a universal byword denoting treachery.

# 8
# Pilate

## The Senseless Washing of His Hands

Closely related to the treachery of Judas, which resulted in Jesus' arrest, was the part played by Pontius Pilate. Both Judas and Pilate were necessary in order for the chief priests and other religious leaders to rid themselves of the man who claimed to be the Messiah.

It was the territory originally ruled by Archelaus, the son of Herod the Great, which in AD 6 was reduced in status and was administered by a series of Roman procurators until AD 41. These leaders had no authority over Roman citizens but were limited to managing the affairs of the nationals of the land in the name of the Empire. During the first twenty years of this period, four different men occupied this most difficult position in hostile Palestine. It was the fifth of these procurators, Pontius Pilate, who came to try his hand at ruling over the Jews.

Like many others appointed by Rome to care for occupied Palestine, Pilate did not fully understand the

Jewish mentality, particularly when it related to the
Mosaic law. His frequent confrontations with this
stubborn people revealed at first a man of rash and
uncompromising actions, but in the end weakness and
inability to exercise his rightful authority.

One of his early conflicts with the religious leaders
was over the issue of emblems displayed in Jerusalem
by the cohort of soldiers assigned to that city. This
particular military contingent happened to have a
human likeness as a part of its insignia, and this they
carried on standards. His predecessors had yielded to
the Jews' wishes in this matter, but Pilate was not so
inclined, probably because he believed his authority
needed to be established early in his tenure as governor. It was unfortunate for him that he chose this issue
upon which to assert the power of his office. The
overthrow of Israel and Judah and the captivity that
followed seemed once and for all to have cured the Jews
of idolatry. The disputed insignia with their imprinted
faces were images absolutely forbidden by Mosaic law,
and the Jews were determined not to allow Gentiles to
desecrate the Holy City. Even at the prospect of being
slaughtered by Pilate's army, they would not give in.
Finally, frustrated by their adamant opposition, he
substituted the force in Jerusalem by one whose
emblems were not offensive. This closed the matter but
resulted in a bad showing for the new man from Rome.

Another incident which greatly disturbed the

Jews was Pilate's appropriation of Temple taxes to build a much-needed aqueduct at Jerusalem. His reasoning was that he would not have to seek funds from Rome if the local community could pay for the project. The serious error was in his use of sacred monies to finance a purely secular enterprise. This time there was no debate, because the Temple authorities kept it a secret until the construction was well underway and it was too late to stop the plan. The results were riots and bloodshed with many of the objectors being killed by Pilate's soldiers.

The Christian world remembers Pilate most for his part in the trial and condemnation to death of Jesus Christ. Almost weekly in many churches this remembrance is corporately recited with the words "suffered under Pontius Pilate." It seems that the events in Pilate's life which preceded his encounter with Christ adequately prepared him for his role in the drama of that morning in the spring of AD 30.

The conspiracy to eliminate Jesus was half complete when Judas's actions in the garden led to the all-night trial culminating in the sentence of death. The interrogation by his accusers was totally ineffective until they brought up his claim of being God's Son. This claim had been the paramount issue all through his public ministry, and now it was the turning point in these proceedings. If this man had not been who he claimed to be, the Jews would have been correct, according to their law, to have judged him deserving of death. After months and months of ignoring the strong evidence that he was who he confessed to be, the priests and other leaders now could do nothing but judge his words to be blasphemous. This they did, and by dawn were ready to approach the Roman authority for permission to execute their prisoner.

It was Passover season in Palestine. Although Pilate's capital was at the port city of Caesarea, this Jewish feast annually brought the governor to Jerusalem to be on hand should there be any uprisings by the people. Religious days for the Jews always brought to mind thoughts of their glorious past. The contrast of their dreams and their present state of submission under the rule of a pagan empire often gave rise to violent acts against the authorities. Managing the city was complicated by the presence of added thousands of visiting pilgrims swelling the city's population. During this time Pilate set up temporary headquarters in Herod's palace, and it was here that those who determined to kill Jesus presented their case. Because the Jews who brought Jesus didn't wish to defile themselves by entering the building, their interview with the governor took place in the court outside.

Wanting to become familiar with the case he was being asked to consider, Pilate's first question was of the nature of the charge being brought against the prisoner. Since any infraction of a religious rule would be of no interest to Pilate and thus end the proceedings, the spokesman replied evasively that they would not have come bringing their prisoner if he were not a criminal. Pilate saw through their subterfuge and suggested they try the accused by their own laws. Of course they had already done this. They reminded Pilate of their inability, under Roman law, to carry out the death penalty, and revealed specifically what they wanted him to do.

Now that he understood their purpose, Pilate seemed more interested and took Jesus into the fortress for a private interview. One of the charges he wished to pursue was Jesus' claim of being the King of the Jews. Along with his desire to keep reasonably peaceful relations with the Jews was an interest in the possibility of someone competing for the position of king. Jesus explained to Pilate that his was a spiritual kingdom and not related to any realm of the real world. Still not quite satisfied with Jesus' answer, Pilate pressed him further about his kingship. Jesus went on to explain that his very birth and life had as its purpose the proclamation of truth, and that everyone who was not deaf to truth would listen. As though to extinguish any spark of understanding that might be kindled, Pilate closed the conversation by wistfully asking "What is truth?" (John 18:38).

Returning to the crowd outside, Pilate reported that his interrogation had not uncovered anything upon which a case could be built. The crowd's response was that the accused had stirred up people all over Judaea, although it had started when he was teaching in Galilee. When Pilate heard that some of this activity had its origin in Galilee, he set about to get Herod Antipas involved, because Galilee was in his jurisdiction, and, therefore, he might be able to dispose of the whole matter, especially if that king business were to come up during questioning. Jesus was then sent to appear before Herod Antipas, who happened to be in the city at the time, and the priests followed to be sure that their case was effectively presented.

Herod had been very curious about Jesus ever since he first heard of him. For a time his superstitious mind allowed him to believe that Jesus was the reincarnation of John the Baptist whom he had beheaded. Now Herod was very eager to see the man, hoping that he would perform some miracle right before his eyes. During the questioning Jesus uttered not one word in spite of the vigorous efforts put forth by his accusers. Since the Jews were desperate for any charge that might stick, one is surprised that they failed to bring up an insulting remark Jesus had made about Herod to a group of Pharisees sometime earlier. The Pharisees had warned Jesus that Herod was out to kill him, and that he should leave the country. Jesus' response was that they should "tell that fox" (Luke 13:32) that the work of casting out devils and curing the sick was going to continue until he had accomplished his goal. After a time of mistreatment by the soldiers in attendance, Jesus was dressed in a purple robe, mocking his claimed royalty, and returned to Pilate.

Once more the problem was literally back on Pilate's doorstep. To make matters worse, while Jesus and his accusers were away Pilate's wife had sent a message warning her husband to have nothing to do with the innocent man who was in his court. She had had a frightening dream about the case which had left her very disturbed.

Again Pilate addressed the crowd, which had reassembled in the courtyard, maintaining that neither he nor Herod could find the prisoner guilty of the charge of subversion. During this exchange Pilate suggested that Jesus be released under the provision of a custom of freeing one accused individual during the festival season. This was probably an annual occurrence instituted as a means of partially pacifying the Jews during those tense religious gatherings. The angry crowd would hear nothing of this plan, but proposed that if anyone were set free it should be the man called Barabbas. Now Barabbas was being held in prison awaiting trial on a number of charges. He had evidently led a group in a minor rebellion against the government and had in the process committed robbery and murder. Since the choice of who would be released was up to the people, Pilate was again frustrated in his efforts to rid himself of this sticky situation. He then asked the crowd, which had now become more aggressive and noisy, what should be done with Jesus. The mob seemed to have been prompted in advance and almost in chorus shouted that Jesus should be crucified. Pilate again tried to find out what crime had been committed, but the sound of his voice was drowned out by shouts of the mob that Jesus be crucified.

It was becoming evident to Pilate that there would be no compromise between the demands of this persistent mob for a guilty verdict and his duty under the law to free the man who he was convinced was innocent. By now the clamor was deafening, and the possibility of a full-scale riot faced Pilate; he would have to make a decision immediately or face the consequences. He quickly called for a basin of water and, in full view of all present, washed his hands as a symbolic gesture of disclaiming any blame for what might happen to Jesus. Pilate may have thought that this act of throwing the responsibility back on the Jews might cause them to reconsider their actions in the light of their own civil as well as religious laws. The figure he used suggesting that his hands were clean of any bloodstains was completely understood and accepted by the mob, for they shouted in response to his act that the blood would be on them and on their children.

Jesus was once more brought into the fortress and was whipped and mistreated by the soldiers. A whipping was carried out with the hope that the painful experience would cause a guilty person to confess to crimes for which there was insufficient evidence. In this case it would have provided Pilate with a much needed solution to his problem. Besides administering the flogging, the soldiers fashioned a crown of thorns and placed it on his head. They put on the robe, which had been removed for the flogging, and probably added a purple mantle. Then the soldiers paid mock homage while repeatedly hitting him in the face.

Pilate went outside and again attested to his belief that there still was no case to be made against the accused. Moments later Jesus emerged wearing the crown of thorns and the "royal" robe. Pilate in a mocking phrase directed toward the mob exclaimed, "Behold the man!" (John 19:5). This infuriated the priests, and again the cries of "Crucify!" were all that could be heard. In desperation, Pilate again shouted back that they should take Jesus and crucify him themselves. Their retort was that his crime was his claim of being the Son of God. Up to that point Pilate had not heard this accusation and now became even more concerned. He went back into the building to question Jesus further.

His first question concerned where Jesus had come from, but to this Jesus gave no answer. This irritated Pilate and he reproved Jesus for refusing to respond, reminding him that being freed or crucified was in the governor's hands. Jesus answered Pilate that what authority he did have over the present situation was not his own but had been granted to him by a higher authority, adding that Pilate's guilt in the affair was less than the guilt of the man who had handed Jesus over to him.

Pilate continued his efforts to release Jesus, but the Jews were so persistent that he finally yielded to their demands. The turning point seems to have been reached when the Jews accused Pilate of disloyalty to the Roman emperor by allowing freedom to a man who claimed to be a king. The political implications of this accusation must have struck home to Pilate, for he then took his official seat in the court and gave permission to carry out the crucifixion of the man he knew to be innocent of any crimes punishable by death. One last sarcastic response by Pilate to the "Crucify!" of the mob was, "Crucify your king?" (John 19:15). To this the crowd shouted back that they had no king but Caesar, and the trial ended.

When Jesus was crucified, Pilate had a sign posted above the cross simply stating the information in three languages that the one hanging there was Jesus of Nazareth King of the Jews. This upset the Jews, and they went to Pilate objecting to what was written. They wanted the sign to read instead "he claimed to be king" (John 19:21, NEB), but Pilate left the inscription as he had originally composed it. A later mention of

Pilate in the Gospel record occurred when he granted Jesus' friends permission to remove his body from the cross and bury it in a tomb just outside the city. And, finally, when the Jews, fearing that some conspiracy might occur concerning Jesus' promise to return from the grave, asked Pilate to secure the grave site with guards, and he granted their request.

Pilate ruled as governor for another six years after the events surrounding the trial and death of Jesus. The dreaded experience of being recalled to Rome for mismanaging his assignment finally came about because of a ruthless and unnecessary show of power against a group of Samaritans. A small band had gathered at the foot of Mount Gerizim with intentions of climbing it in search of some treasure allegedly deposited there by Moses. The assembly was misinterpreted by Pilate as a threat of insurrection. The ensuing attack by his soldiers left numerous casualties, and the result was a formal complaint by the Samaritans to Vitellius, Pilate's superior. He deposed Pilate and ordered him to return to Rome and face charges before the Emperor Tiberius.

Removed from office in disgrace, Pilate set out on the trip to Rome; but before he reached the capital, Tiberius had died. There seems to have been no trial, and the remainder of his life became obscure. One of the persistent traditional stories of those last years is that he lived on a mountain overlooking Lake Lucerne and finally committed suicide by plunging into the lake from a high precipice. This tradition is supported by the fact that the mountain is named Pilatus and that it is often shrouded in fog said to be because of the crime of the infamous man after whom it was named.

If it had not been for his encounter with Jesus Christ, this minor governor of an obscure Roman province might never have been remembered. The time taken up by Jesus' trial before Pilate, although but a forenoon of that fateful day, is detailed by all four of the Gospel writers. It seems to have been very important that Pilate's conflict between the justice he was pledged to uphold and the intense demands of the Jewish leaders receive full coverage in the Scriptures.

Pilate was not only aware of the fact that Jesus was innocent but also understood the hatred and envy that motivated his accusers. This knowledge led him to attempt to get around the death penalty verdict he was being asked to render by repeatedly using an avoidance strategy instead of direct action. Pilate was a mixture of theoretical justice and applied behavior. As long as he maintained a theoretical approach to the situation he was almost a match for the fanatical, sometimes desperate, maneuvers used against Jesus. It was not until someone from the mob shouted a political innuendo that Pilate shifted to the practical side of the question. The unknown heckler may not have realized the importance that Pilate attached to Rome's approval of his administration, especially because his was an appointed position. Some of his past dealings with the Jews had given his superiors cause for concern, and the possible eruption of this current problem might result in his being recalled. He had invested a number of years in his career already. Why should he throw all of this away to rescue one man from death? With these thoughts on his mind, he gave in and allowed the Jews to kill Jesus.

Besides being guilty of betraying his own convictions for political expediency, he appears to have been cruel in allowing the soldiers to have their barbaric fun by unnecessarily abusing their helpless prisoner. This served no purpose other than to satisfy the sadistic appetites of the perpetrators.

Pilate does not seem to be an all-bad villain, but like many villains had the personality flaw that under special circumstances becomes evident. His final disposition of the case in favor of the Jews reversed whatever impression he had tried to convey during the hand-washing display and placed him back into the position of truly being guilty of the body and blood of the King and Messiah of Israel.

# 9
# Herod Agrippa and Son

## The Royal Line of Infamy

Jesus' death by crucifixion occurred around AD 30. This form of Roman execution involved hanging the victim on a cross. The method assured that dying was a slow and painful process put on public display so that the punishment would be a stern reminder for all observers. As had been foretold by Jesus quoting the prophets, his small group of followers had gone their separate ways. It was not until after the resurrection that there began the establishment of a group made up of people who believed Jesus' messianic claim and organized themselves to preach this belief to the world. At first the message was presented to only the Jewish nation as the fulfillment of God's promises to Israel, but Jesus' final instruction just prior to his ascension was that his followers should proclaim the "good news" to all nations. Thus it was that this new and revolutionary religious sect, the church, had its beginnings within the territory still under the domination of Rome. The Book of Acts records the many events in this period of growth along with the interaction of the church with the Roman rulers, Herod Agrippa I, and his son and successor, Herod Agrippa II.

Back in Rome, Tiberius had died and his grand-nephew Caligula became emperor. Caligula's reign lasted only four years and came to an abrupt end with his murder at the hands of his own officers. It was during this period that the three regional divisions of Palestine resulting from the contested will of Herod the Great were consolidated under the rule of Herod Agrippa I. Herod Agrippa I was the son of Aristob-ulus, one of the sons of Herod the Great, who had been put to death during earlier strife in the Herodian family. He was a brother of the infamous Herodias, the woman who caused the death of John the Baptist.

His early years were spent moving from place to place, depending on family and friends for the support of a generally selfish and wasteful life. He had become friends with Caligula before Tiberius died so that when Caligula became emperor the time was right for the rise of this ambitious opportunist to a prominent position in the Empire. Three years earlier his uncle Herod Philip, who was awarded the northern third of Herod the Great's domain, had died and his territory had been temporarily annexed to Syria. Caligula gave this region to Herod Agrippa I, conferred upon him the title of king, and sent him to Palestine.

It was AD 37 when Herod Agrippa I arrived home

to take over his newly acquired land. Herod Antipas was suspicious of his nephew and particularly miffed because the newcomer had the title of "king," which Antipas had never officially been granted although he had served in that capacity nearly forty years. It was his wife, Herodias, who insisted that Herod Antipas go to the Emperor Caligula and request the coveted title. When Herod Antipas went to Rome in AD 39, Agrippa I dispatched one of his men to Rome to accuse his uncle of treason before Caligula. The plan was successful, Herod Antipas was toppled, and the territory including Galilee and Peraea were added to Agrippa's domain.

Two years later the insane Caligula died while Agrippa was visiting Rome. He seems to have been in the right place at the right time, because his assistance to Caligula's successor Claudius netted him the additional territories of Judaea and Samaria. This then made him king over all of the area which had been controlled forty-five years earlier by his grandfather, Herod the Great.

Meanwhile, the fledgling group of believers in Jesus was having great difficulty during the initial stages of development. The Jews who had been successful in having Jesus put to death were now forced to attend to his followers, who continued to claim him as Messiah and to maintain that he had come back from the grave. In addition to opposition from the religious leaders, the young church now experienced persecution from Herod Agrippa I. In support of the Jews' position, he had James beheaded. This was the James who, along with Peter and John, formed the inner circle of the twelve disciples. This trio of followers had witnessed some of the more intimate instances of miracles performed by Jesus. These three men were present when, on the mount of transfiguration, Jesus engaged in a conversation with Moses and Elijah. It was on this occasion that James, John, and Peter actually heard God's voice declaring that Jesus was his Son and that they should listen to him. Herod Agrippa I must have pleased the Jews by eliminating one of the most prominent men in the new movement.

He then went after Peter, another of those who had been with Jesus from the beginning of his ministry. Peter and his brother Andrew had been disciples of John the Baptist, but when they were introduced to Jesus they became his followers. Peter had often been the spokesman for the twelve and now was at the forefront of leadership in the church. Peter was in Jerusalem at the time of Passover, but the festival prevented Herod Agrippa I from carrying out his plans and Peter was put in prison. The king's intention was to make a public display of Peter the day after Passover. Although Peter was assigned sixteen soldiers to prevent his escape, during the night he was miraculously escorted by an angel past the sleeping guards out of the

prison to freedom. Herod Agrippa was so angry to have
failed at this attempt at harassment of the church that
he had all of the soldiers executed for their negligence.

Some time later Herod Agrippa moved to Caesarea where the major military strength of the occupation government was located. One day the king,
dressed in royal garb, was seated on the platform in the
outdoor theater hearing a case involving persons from
another country. During the official proceedings, the
king was so eloquent in his speaking and so resplendent
in the bright sunlight which reflected from his
gorgeous robes that some in the audience were struck
with awe and shouted his praises, exclaiming that it
was not a man, but a god before them. The self-
centered king made no attempt to dissuade the crowd
from their mistaken impression and was immediately
punished by the onslaught of a sudden illness which
resulted in his death a few days later.

This Herod had been king for only six years. He,
like many of his royal relatives, was cruel and ruthless
in his attempts to balance the expectations of Rome and
the dangers of ruling over a people he did not understand. His grandfather, Herod the Great, and his uncle,
Herod Antipas, wrestled with the same problems, and
now he joined them and a long list of other occupation
leaders who lost out to the people who had the superior
God.

Although Agrippa I persecuted the believers

because he thought that his actions would ingratiate himself with the Jewish leaders, the resulting martyr-dom of their key leaders had the effect of adding to the phenomenal growth of the early church. People in large numbers, both Jews and Gentiles, were hearing the gospel of Jesus and responding not only in sincere belief but in giving financial support to those who were called by God and sent out by the church to preach. The work of many of these evangelists was enhanced by miracles of healing and exorcism similar to those which had accompanied Jesus' ministry.

It was in this atmosphere that the third Herodian passed from the scene in a most dramatic manner, dying at the age of fifty-four. His only son, Agrippa II, was too young at seventeen to assume the throne, and so for about six years Palestine was administered by Roman procurators. Emperor Claudius first made the young man king of the small region of Chalcis in the northern part of the country. Three years later his rulership was transferred to the territory including Ituraea and Trachonitis originally held by his great-uncle, Herod Philip. In AD 54 Nero, who had suc-ceeded Claudius as emperor, added Galilee and Peraea to the realm of Herod Agrippa II, so that he ruled over an area roughly equal to two thirds of that of his great-grandfather, Herod the Great. The remainder of the area, Judaea and Samaria, were under procurators during those years.

The times were very unsettled. Nero had come to power in Rome through the efforts of his mother Agrippina. She convinced her husband Claudius to name her son by a previous marriage as his successor and then poisoned him, ushering in the sixth and last of the line of Caesars. It was Nero who had many Christians in Rome killed as punishment for the destructive fire of AD 64 which he himself may have ordered set. Later he had his mother killed and finally in AD 68 took his own life. In Palestine the conflict between the Jewish priests and the followers of the Christian movement was beginning to involve the Roman authorities.

There was a Pharisee named Saul who was a very zealous antagonist of the Christians. His religious fervor led him to dedicate his efforts to stamp out this new "Way," as it was called. On one of his assignments to jail believers of the city of Damascus, he had a most extraordinary experience which changed him so completely that the remainder of his life was spent proclaiming the gospel as the most famous missionary of the biblical record. About the same time he went through this radical change he took the name Paul. His work was so effective that the Jews were continually frustrated and embarrassed that one of their very promising young men would turn out to be a most formidable preacher and spokesman for the Christian religion.

As in the case of Jesus of Nazareth, the Jewish leaders made every effort to either kill Paul themselves or get him in trouble with the Roman authorities. It was on one such occasion that the last of our villains, Herod Agrippa II, and this famous hero of the church crossed paths. It was after a number of successful missionary trips that Paul returned to Jerusalem, and his presence in the city caused no small stir. This time a false charge against him of bringing Gentiles into the Temple set the whole town into turmoil. A mob dragged Paul from the Temple and would have stoned him, except that the uproar attracted the attention of the authorities who upon quelling the riot rescued him.

Suspecting that the central character of the disturbance must be guilty of something, the commandant ordered that he be examined by flogging. As Paul was being secured, he revealed that he was a Roman citizen, and that it would be a breach of Roman law to subject a citizen to the whip. Paul was a Roman citizen by birth. Although he was a Jew of the tribe of Benjamin, his father probably was awarded citizenship for some service to Rome and he had passed this status along to his son. The issue of Paul being a Roman quickly brought the proceedings to a halt, and he was placed in protective custody.

The days that followed brought no decision concerning his case. Paul's accusers made various charges against him, both religious and civil, none of which were very strong. Since releasing him would mean certain death and because one of the charges was sedition, it was decided to move the prisoner to Caesarea, the capital city.

During the next two years, Paul languished in the prison at Caesarea. His accusers came from Jerusalem to follow up their case, but the entire matter was at a standstill. Felix, the procurator of Judaea, was interested in Paul and from time to time would hear the pros and cons of the case but was unable to arrive at any adequate disposition. Eventually Felix was replaced by Porcius Festus who to keep the Jews partially satisfied continued Paul's imprisonment. Once again the priests made their appearance before the court at Caesarea, but on this occasion Paul invoked his right as a Roman citizen to appeal to Nero, and Festus was obliged to begin plans for the trip to Rome.

It happened a few days later, before Paul left for Italy, that Herod Agrippa II along with his sister Bernice made a courtesy visit to Festus. The incestuous relationship between the king and his sister was well known, for they openly lived together. She had been married twice, but after the death of her second husband returned to the scandalous union she had had with her brother before her first marriage.

Partly because it would be a nice gesture to ask his guest's advice on Paul's case and also because the king was knowledgeable about Jewish religious matters,

Festus asked the king if he would talk with Paul before he was sent to the emperor. The idea appealed to Agrippa and so the next day with Festus, Bernice and a group of dignitaries, Paul was brought into the hall to present his defense. Festus opened the proceedings by introducing Paul and the details of the case to the assembly. He explained as much as he knew about the charges brought by the Jews and indicated that before he sent the prisoner on to Rome, he hoped that this hearing before Agrippa would provide more information for his written report. Finally, Agrippa extended an invitation to Paul to address the group and present his answer to the Jews' allegations.

Paul's entire speech was directed toward Agrippa, probably because he understood Jewish history and the prophecies surrounding the promised coming of Messiah. To emphasize by contrast his present spiritual dedication, Paul told of the almost fanatical zeal with which he had earlier persecuted those who claimed that Jesus of Nazareth was the Messiah. He went on to detail his own experience of accepting this truth and of being commissioned by Christ to preach that men's eyes would be opened so that they would not be dominated by Satan, and that trust in Christ would result in the forgiveness of sins. He said that this preaching, which so upset the Jews that they were trying to do away with him, was based squarely upon what was foretold by the prophets (i.e., that the

Messiah must suffer, die, and rise from the dead to announce a new age for both Jews and Gentiles).

Festus, who by now was completely astonished by Paul's assertions because he could not grasp their meaning, suddenly cried out that Paul's intellectual pursuits had left his mind in a state of madness. Paul's answer to Festus was that he was not mad, and that the facts he had been giving were in the open and easily accessible to all. Once again addressing Agrippa, he asked him directly if he believed the prophets. But before the king could reply, Paul interjected the answer that he was sure the king did believe the prophetic sayings. Agrippa did not refute this answer, but responded with the notion that even if he did accept what the prophets said, he was still not persuaded to become a Christian. After this exchange, the hearing was ended with the principals unable to support the Jews' contention. Because Paul had requested presentation of his case before the emperor at Rome, which was his right under Roman law, plans were set in motion to sail to Italy.

We do not know what finally happened to this fourth, and last, Herod. He is cited here not so much because of his bad conduct, albeit he was a "Herodian," but because of his response to Paul's testimony.

In the study of the last of our bad characters, we find in Agrippa's interrogation of Paul some light shed on the answer to the question of what can be done about evil behavior. Although the hearing before Agrippa was held primarily to supply Festus with information, it soon became evident that it was a conversation between two men. At the same time Paul was defending his actions, he was reviewing for Agrippa what he had discovered in God's plan for his human creation. He explained that the plan took many years to unfold, and during those years God preserved a special nation in which his nature and purposes would be revealed and from which his son Jesus would emerge to fulfill all of the promises.

The sermon, if it can be called that, did not take up specific deeds perpetrated by Agrippa which would easily characterize him as a "bad" person. Not even the presence of Agrippa's sister Bernice with its obvious implications tempted Paul to allude to the particular sins of his listeners. What he did emphasize was that a correct understanding of who Jesus was and what he did was sufficient to bring a person, any person, to a very important decision. Paul challenged Agrippa to make the final step in faith by believing in Jesus on the basis of what Paul knew Agrippa understood. His answer, whether given for political or personal reasons, was a definite negative, stopping at the very brink of receiving God's promised forgiveness of his sins and a sure place of eternal presence with him.

The villains of the Old and New Testament force us to observe a very disturbing side of our human state.

The Bible gives an unvarnished picture of real people so that each of us can see in himself or herself the potential for wrongdoing. But it also provides the remedy, which is not a be-as-good-as-you-can solution, but rests upon what one believes. The wonder of it is that the same God who established the laws and rules by which man is judged has also provided the means by which man is able to be in harmony with this requiring God. Unlike the plants and animals, we are destined to make choices in the light of what we believe about God and his expectations over against the dictates of our own judgments. The important point which was missed by Herod Agrippa II was that one begins with correct beliefs based on God's revelation. Like King Agrippa, most of us are not lacking in basic information concerning the facts surrounding religious issues. The problem for many is that they do not have enough confidence in the facts to warrant a full and complete surrender to what God wants.

The plan alluded to in the Old Testament, which promised a Messiah who would bless Israel, is fully illuminated in the New Testament with the life, death, and resurrection of Christ. For bad men who wish to change their present life and future destiny, the invitation continues to be proclaimed by the God of Abraham, Isaac, and Jacob through their most illustrious descendant—Jesus of Nazareth.